What Granny Didn't Tell Me

MICHAEL K PETRIE

TO MY FAMILY

To my family, past and present. To all the story tellers who spend countless hours digging into their family's history in a relentless effort to record the individual human stories of our past that make us who we are today.

.

CONTENTS

CHAPTER THREE
Back Up The Tree

CHAPTER FOUR
English Connection

ACKNOWLEDGMENTS

This compilation of stories about the Petrie family would not have been possible without the many comments and suggestions from relatives and friends. Special mention to Peter Lyn, Lorraine Morgan, Lesley-Ann Petrie, Elizabeth Rowland and Janice Watson for their input and ideas. I'd also like to acknowledge my appreciation to Sylvia Dorey for keeping me on track.

Material and content for this book have come from many sources. Every attempt has been made to ensure its accuracy. However, many of the records consulted were transcribed from hand written documents, in some cases, going back hundreds of years. Inevitably, transcription mistakes were made or information was incomplete. Nevertheless, I have tried to find multiple sources for dates and events where possible so I am reasonably comfortable with the facts that I report.

.

INTRODUCTION

When I was growing up in the 1950s and 60s, I had the privilege of spending a short time, before she died with my paternal grandmother, Margaret Petrie (Grandma Petrie). I was fascinated by her broad brogue (Scottish accent). It was so different from the rest of my family. She didn't own a television, so when I would spend a few days staying with her, every night was filled with stories about Rutherglen where she came from in Scotland and tales of her native land. It sounded so romantic and far off.

In 1958, she took me to see Wee Geordie, a film about a bodybuilder who competed in the 1956 Olympic Games for Scotland. Everyone in the movie sounded like Grandma Petrie and she assured me that all the scenes in Scotland portrayed the Scotland she remembered fondly.

I learned a lot about where she grew up and the lore of Scotland but when I asked about the history of the Petrie family, she replied there isn't much to tell. The Petries, after all, were just a poor immigrant family who came to Canada looking for a better life. So, what's there to tell. But I always suspected there was more to the Petrie story that she did not share.

CHAPTER ONE

THE PETRIES

EPISODE 1

IN THE BEGINNING

T oday, there are Petries all over the world. By far the majority are still in Scotland but through many years of Scottish emigration, the Petrie name can be found in almost any country in the world with large concentrations in the United States, Canada, Australia and New Zealand. Most genealogists believe the name was established in the northeast of Scotland from Flemish roots and grew in popularity during the proscription of the Clan MacGregor in the 17th century. For more details see my story about the MacGregors in the next episode.

Traders from Antwerp

Some think the Petries of Scotland originated from a Flemish family named Peters that had migrated from Antwerp to Cornwall in the 12th century. From there the family moved to the northeast of Scotland ending up in Aberdeenshire. This is probably true because Scotland was looking to weaving as an important part of its economy and the Flemish were renowned for their weaving skills. The weaving industry played a major economic role in the northeast of Scotland for several centuries.

Petrie is the diminutive form of the given name Peter and Patrick and appears in early records in and around Aberdeen as Petrie, Patre, Petre, Petrye, Paitre, Patrie and Patry. The first recorded spelling of the name is that of Charles Patre. It

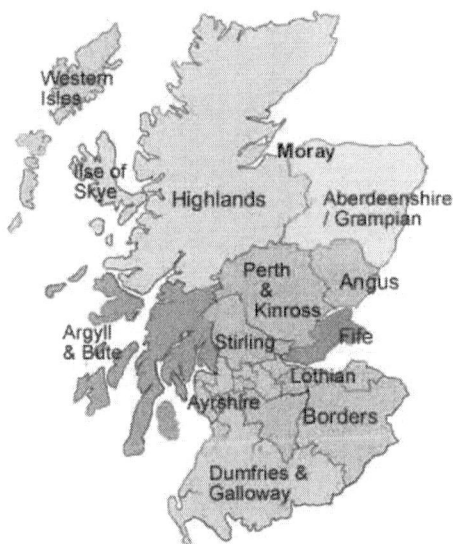

was found in the Balwelow Records for Aberdeen in 1513. Between 1570 and 1620 the name appears more frequently in church records and is slowly moving south into Angus. Clusters of Petries were found in Dundee and Monifieth in Angus, St. Nicholas in Aberdeen and Elgin in Moray.

During the 1600s the majority of Petrie names appeared in Angus with smaller clusters in Aberdeen, Fife and in the Shetland Islands. The migration south from Aberdeenshire and Moray counties to Angus and Fife makes sense but where does Shetland come in? During the 17th century many people were displaced from their homes as part of the "Clearances", a plan by the English landlords who owned great chunks of Scotland to evict the tenants from their lands to make way for improved agricultural activities and new industry. Many were forced into the cities and towns looking for work or were forced to emigrate. Some Petrie families, it is believed, left the Aberdeen area looking for work and headed north to the Shetland Islands. They had developed skills in the production of "tang" which is the processing of seaweed and the Shetlands had plenty of seaweed. Tang is produced when seaweed is processed and the extract is used in the production of soap and glass. This was a big deal in the 17th century.

Today, almost all Petries around the world can trace their roots back to these Scottish regions. There may be a few exceptions that probably stem from the Flemish trade with other parts of Europe back in the 12th and 13th centuries. The Scots have always been adventurous people, willing to travel great distances for discovery and economic gain. During the many years of conflict with England, Scottish traders were constantly looking for new markets in Europe and elsewhere. So, it is no surprise that there are now more Scots living outside of Scotland than within. While many Petries come from the same roots or backgrounds we are not all related genetically. As DNA testing becomes more popular, we may get a better picture of the relationships between the Petries.

EPISODE 2

THE MACGREGORS

When I tell people that my name is Petrie, I often hear that must be French or Italian, or maybe Belgian. Well, actually the name does come from Flanders, but more on that later. I always respond, no we Petries are Scottish through and through and our Gaelic roots go back hundreds of years.

A Petrie is really a MacGregor. The surname Petrie is a sept or assumed name of the surname MacGregor. The clan

MacGregor or Gregor first appears in records in the 12th century in Scotland taking their name from an ancient ancestor, Gregor of the early royal Celtic tribe of Alpia. An interesting side note; the clan is known as the first to play bagpipes in Scotland in the early 17th century. For which we are all so grateful.

The MacGregors' traditional lands were Glenstrae, Glenlochy and Glenorchy. As a reward for service to Scotland, King David II, son of Robert The Bruce gave Glenorchy, the ancient seat of the MacGregors to the clan Campbell. The MacGregors were loathed to leave, but by 1400 the MacGregor chiefship had moved to Glenstrae. (on Loch Awe, northwest of Glasgow in the Scottish Highlands). However, their troubles were only beginning.

The Campbells were great ones for using the law against those whose lands they coveted. Their method was to provoke the MacGregors to acts of violence, (not especially difficult, given the MacGregor temper) and then invoke the law to put them down and take their lands. By this method, the Campbells ripped clan MacGregor of their Glenlyon holding in 1502. Things came to a head when in 1589 the MacGregor clan chief murdered John Drummond, King, James VI's forester. In 1603, the King issued an edict of "fire and sword", proclaiming the name MacGregor abolished. Those having the name MacGregor were told to renounce their name or be hanged. MacGregors were hunted down, primarily by Campbells who placed a bounty on their heads and bred bloodhounds specifically to hunt and kill MacGregors. The clan was scattered and became known as the "Children of the Mist".

The original proscription law which was passed by the Scottish Parliament in 1617 stated:

"It was ordained that the name MacGregor should be abolished and that the whole persons of that name should renounce their name and take some other name and that they nor none of their name and that they nor none of their posterity should call themselves Gregor or MacGregor under pain of death…that any person or persons of the said clan who has already renounced their names or hereafter shall renounce their names or if any of their children or posterity shall at any time hereafter assume or take themselves the name Gregor or MacGregor… that every such person or persons assuming or taking to themselves the said name…shall incur the pain of death which pain shall be executed upon them without favour."

Clan members were forced to adopt other names to save their lives. One of the names adopted was Petrie and MacPetrie.

Rob Roy MacGregor

During this period, a notable MacGregor emerged. Rob Roy MacGregor was born in 1671, a younger son of MacGregor of Glengyle. However, he used his mother's maiden name, Campbell for most of his life to avoid persecution. To avenge his ancestors and protect his own land, Rob Roy became an outlaw and cattle rustler. His adventures were immortalized by Sir Walter Scott in his novel Rob Roy. He proved to be a thorn in the side of the government until he died in 1734.

Despite the brutal treatment of the MacGregors, they nevertheless fought for the king during the Scottish Civil War. In recognition of this Charles II Stewart of England repealed the proscription of the name. When Charles's brother James VII was deposed by William of Orange, the MacGregors became Jacobites and fought for the restoration of a Stewart to the throne, Charles Edward Stewart (Bonnie

Prince Charlie). After the defeat of the Jacobite highland clans at the battle of Littleferry and Culloden, the name MacGregor was once again banned by William of Orange.

During the proscription, many MacGregors moved east to the area around Aberdeen where Flemish traders were frequent visitors. The Flemish name for Peter or Patrick was Petrie which was quickly taken up by MacGregors with the name Peter or Patrick.

The persecution of the clan MacGregor lasted until 1774 when the laws against them were repealed. By that point, the Petrie sept of clan MacGregor was well established and flourishes until today.

After George III finally annulled the law prohibiting the name MacGregor, the clan chose a new Chief, General John Murray of Lanrick. Murray was a MacGregor descended from Duncan MacGregor of Ardchoille, who had died in 1552.

The current Chief of Clan MacGregor is Sir Malcolm Gregor Charles MacGregor of MacGregor, 24th Chief of Clan MacGregor. Sir Malcolm and Lady MacGregor currently live in Bannatyne, Newtyle in Scotland, just in case you want to drop by for tea.

Sir Malcolm & Lady MacGregor

EPISODE 3

✦P✦

FORFARSHIRE 1636 - 1720

During my genealogy hunt, the first Petrie relative I discovered, my 7th great grandfather, was Georg Petrie. He was born during the reign of Charles Stuart (King Charles I) on August 18, 1636, in an ancient, small village in Forfarshire (now the county of Angus) called Arbirlot. The village is located approximately 2.5 miles from the town of Arbroath on the east coast of Scotland and 24 miles north of

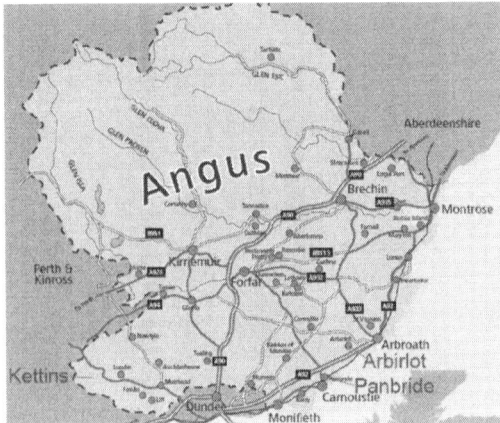

Dundee. There is evidence of prehistoric occupation of the area around Arbirlot including a Druid temple and Roman marching camp. In the 1600s when Georg was born the village was part of the Barony of Kellie controlled by the Irvines of Drum.

Records of Georg's parents are sketchy but his father's name may have been Hendrie Petrie. The family more than likely were tenants living on the land of the Irvine family employed as farmers and in the early weaving trade which would have included a loom in their stone croft. The area in south Angus and into Fife was just starting to develop as the centre of the jute weaving industry in Scotland. It would become one of the most important occupations in the area during the 18th and 19th centuries.

On July 16, 1670, George married Isabell Smith who was born in Arbirlot in October 1638. Her father, my 8th great grandfather is listed as Jhone Smith with no further details. They had at least three children; Margaret Petrie (1671-1753), Alexander Petrie, my 6th great grandfather (1674) and Isabell Petrie (1679) all born within 20 miles of Arbirlot which suggests the family moved from farm to farm looking for work. Although no detailed records of when they died have been located, George and Isabell died in Panbride, Angus sometime after 1680. In those days, it was not uncommon for poor families to not have a gravestone or use a wooden marker which over time would deteriorate to nothing.

Alexander Petrie was born in Kettins, Angus, a small hamlet about 24 miles northwest of Dundee. Around 1680 the family moved to Panbride, a small village about half a mile from the east coast and six miles south of Arbroath in Angus. There Alexander met Isobel Miln who was born in Panbride in 1680. Alexander and Isobel married in 1699. However, it appears they had two children out of wedlock, Andrew Petrie, my 5th great grandfather (1696-1754) and David Petrie (1697-). They went on to have four more children; Henry Petrie (1706-), Helen Petrie (1709-), John Petrie (1709-) and Suzanna Petrie (1726-). The family lived in Panbride until 1720 when they moved to Dundee.

As you can imagine records from this time are sketchy with many people having similar names. For example, there are several Alexander Petries in parish records that were born around the same period and in the same area of Angus. All of them had sons named Andrew. Therefore, it may be possible that Andrew, my 5th great grandfather may have had different parents. However, I am sticking with Alexander and Isobel as they appear to be the pick of other genealogists I've consulted with.

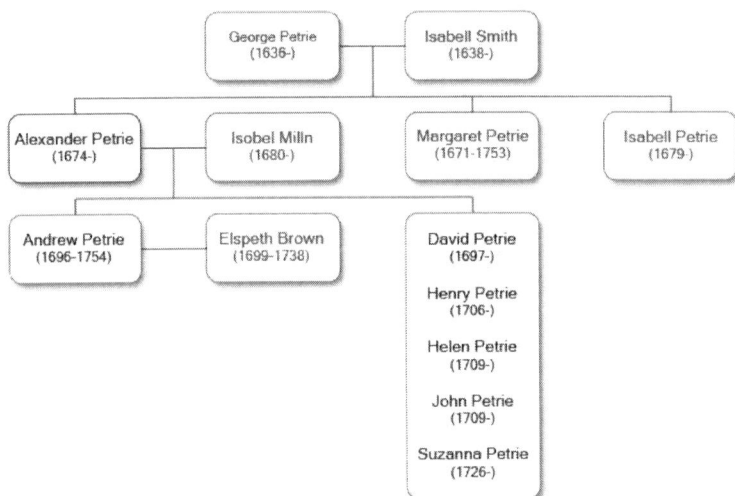

EPISODE 4

~🙟P🙝~

MONIKIE 1721 -1754

Andrew Petrie met Elspeth Brown from Monikie Parish, Angus in 1720 and they were married on November 23, 1721, in Monikie where the couple decided to live. Andrew got a job working on the estate of the Lord of Panmure at Panmure House just outside the hamlet of Monikie. Lord Panmure had been exiled in 1716 to France because of his

Panmure House

support for the Jacobite cause. Panmure House had just been renovated and was considered one of the finest country homes in all of Scotland. Despite their inability to live there, the Maule family (Earls of Panmure) wanted to ensure the house was maintained and ready for them when and if they were able to return. It's not clear what exactly Andrew Petrie did at Panmure or if, in fact, he even lived in the house. It was a big step up from being a tenant farmer or weaver like his ancestors.

Andrew and Elspeth had six children; William Petrie (1725-1797), James Petrie (1727-1797), Andrew Petrie (1730-), Ann Petrie (1731-), Jean Petrie (1731-) and my 4th great grandfather John Petrie (1737-).

At some point, Andrew left his employment at Panmure and along with his extended family took up the weaving trade.

Monikie Today

Monikie was becoming known for its "Osnaburgh" weaving which is coarse brown linen due to the low grade of flax grown in the area. The Petries worked closely with the Hog family of Loanhead in Monikie parish who were know, at the time to be the most successful weaving family in the area with one of the largest looms available at the time. In fact, Andrew's grandson John Petrie (1760-1824) married into the Hog family.

Monikie Kirkyard

At some point, Andrew became a "merchant – turner" which is similar to a wholesaler, probably as part of the weaving trade. During the 1730s he made several trips to the Shetland Islands off the north coast of Scotland where in 1754 he died.

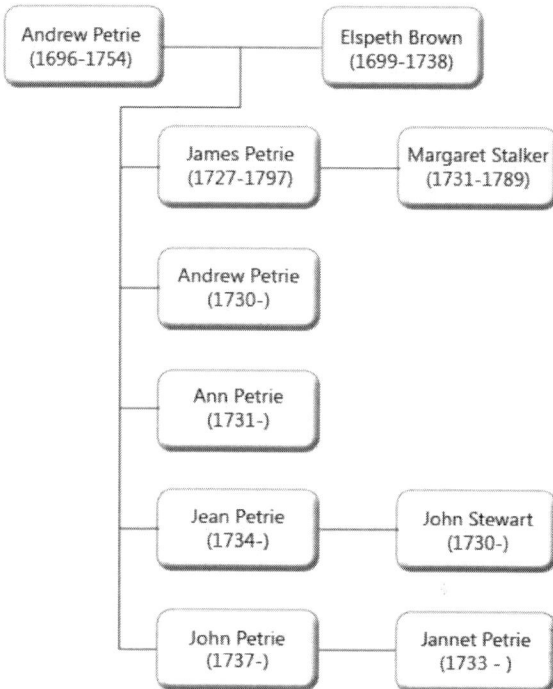

EPISODE 5

⁓❦P❧⁓

THE JACOBITES

Now, a bit of Scottish history to put things in perspective. The Stewart/Stuart period in British history lasted from 1603 to 1714. The period was plagued with religious strife and a civil war that saw the execution of King Charles I and the abolishment of the monarchy under Oliver Cromwell, which lasted for 11 years. In 1660

Oliver Cromwell

Cromwell's regime collapsed and CharlesII assumed the throne. His Catholic brother, James II followed in 1685. He was overthrown in 1689 in the "Glorious Revolution" by his Protestant daughter Mary, and her husband William of Orange. For the next 50 years the exiled James II and his son James Francis Edward Stuart and his grandson Charles Edward Stuart, "Bonnie Prince

James II

Charlie", claimed that they were the true kings of Scotland and England. Through numerous unsuccessful attempts to return to power, their supporters became known as "Jacobites".

The Jacobites could be found throughout the British Isles but were most numerous in the highlands and the northeast of Scotland particularly among those of the Roman Catholic faith. The county of Angus, or Forfarshire, made significant contributions to the Jacobite cause including the family of Andrew Petrie, my 5th great grandfather. In 1743, Bonnie Prince Charlie raised an army of Scottish clans and attempted to take the British throne from King George II. Despite early victories, they were ultimately defeated at the bloody Battle of Culloden on April 16, 1746.

Bonnie Prince Charlie

The bonnie Prince escaped to the Isle of Skye with the help of Flora MacDonald who disguised him as her maid. From Skye, he eventually made it to the continent where he spent the rest of his life. Culloden was the last time Scotland and England were to fight each other.

At the age of 18, Andrew Petrie's son James, my 5th great uncle joined the Jacobite regiment known as the Forfarshire Regiment under the leadership of Lord Ogilvy. James survived the battle of Culloden but was captured shortly thereafter by the English and held for almost two years in jail at Carlisle. Following a brief trial, he was sentenced to death by hanging or transportation to the West Indies as an indentured slave. Despite being a life sentence, he chose "transportation" to Jamaica. The life expectancy of a

European indentured slave was short and hard. They were very susceptible to tropical diseases which made slaves from Africa, being more acclimated, much more desirable to work in the West Indies.

On May 5, 1747, James set sail along with 150 other Jacobite prisoners on the HMS Veteran to Antigua, St. Kitts and Jamaica. The crossing, according to the ship's log went well until the day before they

Diamond Attacking HMS Veteran

were scheduled to arrive in Antigua. Unprepared, the ship was attacked by a French ship, the Diamond. The French ship, after a short engagement, under the command of Captain Paul Marsale claimed victory and took control of the English ship.

Le Compte de Caylus

The Diamond took the prisoners to the French island of Martinique where they were released and subsequently given their freedom by the island's governor, le Compte de Caylus. When news of this reached the British Government, they wrote to the Governor demanding that he return the prisoners to the British. The Governor of Martinique, having received the letter six months after the prisoners had been given their liberty refused the request.

Many of the freed prisoners became French subjects, some heading to France while others stayed on in Martinique, where their relatives can be found to this day. A few including James Petrie decided to go home to Scotland. He eventually made it back to Monikie where he married Margaret Stalker. She was also from Monikie and they had five children.

EPISODE 6

ANGUS TO FIFE

My 4th great grandfather John Petrie was born in 1737 in either Monikie in Angus or Yell in the Shetland Islands. We know that John's father and mother travelled to Yell and he may have been born there. Records show baptisms for both locations. However, I suspect he was born in Monikie. While a young man, John moved south from Angus into the county of Fife. He was probably looking for work or travelling with family members. He appears to have settled for a while in the area just south of Kirkcaldy near the east coast of Fife. Fishing was an important trade in the area and he may have actually travelled south from Angus by fishing boat.

I would like to provide a little background on the county of Fife and why someone in the late 1700s would move there. Fife, is bounded to the north by the Firth of Tay and to the south by the Firth of Forth. It is a natural peninsula whose political boundaries have changed little over the ages. Originally, a Pictish kingdom, the county is still known as the

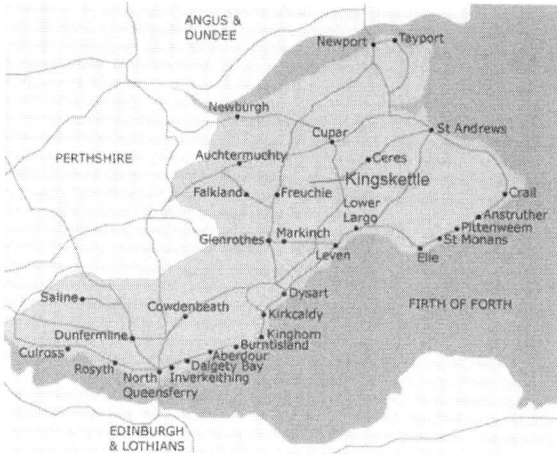

Kingdom of Fife. Fife was an important royal and political centre for several hundred years with royal residences in Dunfermline and Falkland.

The northern part of the county is rich agricultural land where flax for the linen trade was a major crop. The southern part of Fife became more industrialized in the 19th century. Coal had been mined in the area since the 12th century, but the number of pits increased ten-fold as the demand for coal grew during the Victorian period. Fishing was viable from numerous small ports along the east coast combined with the production of salt. So, there were lots of opportunities for someone looking for work.

According to church records, John Petrie married Jannet Kilgoure in 1749 in Kinghorn, Fife. I am a bit confused about these dates as John would have been 13 or 14 when he got married and Jannet would have been 16. Early teen marriages, although not common did exist in the 1700s, talk about robbing the cradle. Although the records look solid, they were handwritten and may have been based on word of mouth or second-hand information. Jannet was born in Burntisland, about two miles south of Kinghorn. Together they had at least two children; Elizabeth (1752-) and William (1754 – 1816), my 3rd great grandfather.

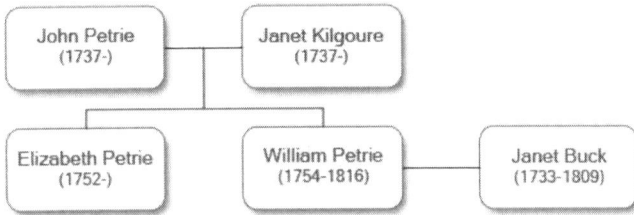

John more than likely was a farm labourer and moved around the southeast part of Fife depending on the work available. The area is rich agricultural land and work would have been plentiful and usually came with lodging. There are no records of when or where John or Jannet died but it probably was in the same area of Fife.

William Petrie lived and worked with his parents until he was in his early twenties. At that point, he set out looking for work around Fife and ended up in Kingskettle, Fife. I suspect he entered into an arrangement as an apprentice to one of the established linen weavers in Kettle. Apprenticeships usually lasted between six and seven years. That might explain why he married at a reasonably mature age for the time at 36. In Kingskettle he met Janet Buck, originally from the Scottish Lowlands, Kirknewton, south of Edinburgh. Janet's parents were also farmers and had lived in Kirknewton all their lives. Janet probably left home looking for work as a domestic and ended up in Kingskettle. William and Janet were married in 1790 in Kingskettle and moved into a house in Bankton Park which was a hamlet adjacent to Kingskettle where the family stayed for three generations. The 1841 and subsequent census reports show that the Petries lived at #7 Bankton Park which by then was part of Kingskettle.

Kingskettle Today

Kingskettle is also known as Kettle. However, Kettle is actually the parish where Kingskettle is located and many of the small villages and hamlets are also referred to in many documents as just Kettle. The parish is relatively small, located in central Fife, three-quarters of a mile east of the village of Ladybank, six miles southwest of the city of Cupar and 28 miles northeast of Edinburgh. Originally called Catul or Katel, a name supposed to refer to the site of an ancient battle. The area was part of a royal hunting preserve, hence the name Kingskettle. The area is considered fertile and ideal for the cultivation of flax, essential for the linen trade. There were also limited deposits of coal in the parish which contributed to limited early industrialization.

Kingskettle, Kettlebridge, and Bankton Park are all within one square mile and as mentioned are usually referred to as just Kettle.

EPISODE 7

‹P›

GENERATIONS OF WEAVERS

Weaving and the production of linen was an important part of the lives of the Petries in Angus and Fife. So, I thought a little background might be helpful.

Weaving had been a fairly common occupation during the medieval period in Scotland. The skills were taught to apprentices by master weavers belonging to the local or regional weaving guild. For example, one of the largest guilds was in Dundee and set the standards for the production of linen for several centuries. This remained the normal way of teaching skilled trades right up to the industrial revolution.

In 1587, the Scottish Parliament passed an Act intended to encourage skilled Flemish weavers to move to Scotland, to develop the local skills base in Scotland. However, the Flemish weavers could only take on Scottish children as apprentices even if it meant foregoing their own children learning the trade. An apprenticeship usually started at the age of 12 to 14 and would last for six or seven years. This was usually without pay but in many cases included board and meals. At the end of the apprentice period, the weaver became a journeyman and, in a few cases progressed to the status of master. The creation of new master weavers was a rare event and, in most cases, they were relatives of existing masters. In Kingskettle, there may have only been one master weaver at any given period up until the industrial revolution.

Stooks of Flax

In researching how linen was produced I was impressed by how hard my relatives must have worked to earn a living. The production of linen starts with the cultivation of flax which has a fibrous stalk that when woven produces a sturdy, long-lasting material. The arable land in Angus and Fife was ideal for the growing of flax and not much else. Since before the 16th century the production of linen cloth had been the main source of local employment. That was until 1815 when French prisoners from the Napoleonic wars were used to drain the bogs in central Fife and more profitable crops could be introduced. At this point more and more flax had to be imported from Russia and the Netherlands.

Retting Flax

The next stages of linen production were the reaping of the flax, retting the flax plants, scutching, spinning, weaving, bleaching and dyeing. Sounds complicated.

After the flax has been harvested it goes into a retting pit which is basically a bog filled with dirty water. In the bog, a very stinky fermentation process takes place which breaks down the fibres. The more stagnant the water, the quicker the fibres break down.

The next stage of production was scutching, an energetic beating process of passing the fibre through rollers to break it up further. This was followed by hackling which involved using a

Hackling and Spinning Flax

wooden comb to smooth the fibres out and remove the seeds. Women then spun the fibre into yarn before it was woven into cloth, bleached and dyed. In 1840 women were paid up to five shillings for spinning and men earned 12 for doing the weaving. Pay inequity existed even then for broadly similar work, funny that.

Hand Loom

The late 18th century saw the introduction of mechanized spinning and the transformation of a cottage industry to local mills powered by steam. The commercial production of linen by families like the Petries using home-grown flax was no longer economically viable by the 1830s. This was due primarily to the increasing competition from linen woven locally in larger premises using yarn machine-spun in mills from imported flax and, an increase of cheaper linen production in Ireland. However, the transformation took several years during which many families continued to weave linen on their home looms using yarn supplied by the local mills. In 1834, there were 378 hand-looms still in operation in Kettle parish alone including the Petrie family living at number 7 Bankton Park.

Arthurfield Linen Mill, Kettle

In 1850, the Beveridge family of Kingskettle opened the Arthurfield Works mill and in 1870 another mechanized mill was opened in the neighbouring village of Freuchie. Both of these mills remained in operation until the 1930s.

The production of linen also became more specialized with finer material being produced in larger mills in main towns such as Dundee and Dunfermline while courser types of cloth were being produced in places such as Kingskettle. These rougher materials classified as Dowlas, Silesias, Osnaburgs were used for sail canvas, bed-ticks, window blinds and other forms of sheeting materials. An interesting side note; sailcloth from Fife was often used to cover wagons, such as those used in the opening of the American frontier. When the wagons finished their trek across the prairies and were no longer needed, there was no waste. An inspired gentleman bought the material and cut it up to make tough trousers for the miners of California. His name was Levi Strauss and he gave the world denim.

In time the Petrie weavers transitioned from their cottage-based weaving to working in one of the mills and eventuallylooked for other forms of work.

EPISODE 8

WILLIAM PETRIE & JANET BUCK

William Petrie and Janet Buck had six children; James Petrie (1791-1886), William Petrie (1793-) David Petrie (1795-1800), Andrew Petrie (1796-1865), John Petrie (1798-1871) and my 2nd great grandfather David Petrie (1804-1870). Janet died in 1809 and a year later William married Margaret Wilkie (1775-1816), as he needed someone to take care of his children. They had a further four children; Janet Petrie (1810-1895), George Butchert Petrie (1812-1891), Robert Petrie (1814-1895), and Mathie Petrie (1816-1869). It appears that Margaret may have died in childbirth with son Mathie. All of the children were born in Bankton Park and lived all their lives within the parish of Kettle. Most were also involved in linen weaving with son James taking over the ownership of the house and loom at Bankton Park. Sons, William and John became farmers in the area.

The house in Bankton Park originally was a two-room stone cottage. One room was used for the linen loom and the other is where the family lived. Over time the house was expanded

Bankton Park House Today

to include a separate loom shed out back enabling more people to live in the house proper. The house still exists and has been modernized into a three-bedroom bungalow. It appears to have been combined with the house next door, #5 Bankton Park. The loom shed is still there.

Several years ago, I visited the old cemetery in Kingskettle looking for Petrie graves. I was sure there would be many but was surprised to find only one, my 3rd great uncle, Andrew Petrie. I'm told that as many families of the time, the Petries were too poor to afford stone grave markers. A wooden cross would have been sufficient and by now they have all rotted away. If you are ever in that area and want to do a little grave hunting, the church office does have a map where all are buried. Be assured that the Petries are all still there.

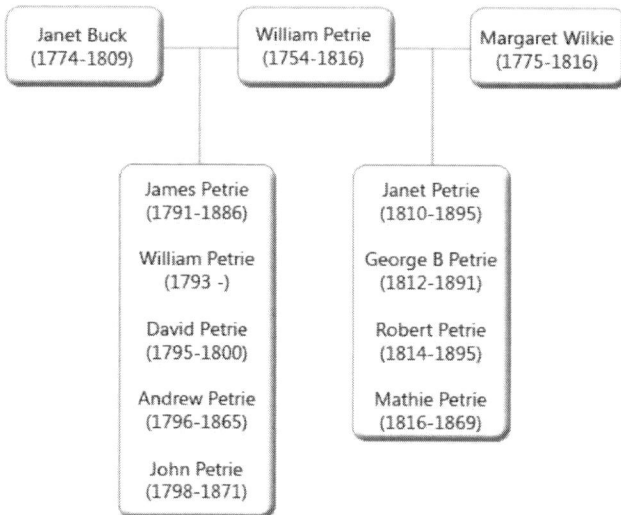

Janet Buck (1774-1809)	William Petrie (1754-1816)	Margaret Wilkie (1775-1816)

James Petrie (1791-1886)	Janet Petrie (1810-1895)
William Petrie (1793 -)	George B Petrie (1812-1891)
David Petrie (1795-1800)	Robert Petrie (1814-1895)
Andrew Petrie (1796-1865)	Mathie Petrie (1816-1869)
John Petrie (1798-1871)	

EPISODE 9

GOD SAVE THE KING

David Petrie, my 2nd great grandfather was born in Kingskettle in 1804. He was named after a brother who had died at the age of five in 1800. He followed his father and brother James in the handloom linen trade in their Bankton Park cottage. In 1831 he married Helen Dalrymple from Markinch, Fife, about five miles from Kingskettle. Helen's family had lived in the Markinch area since at least 1710 and most were farmers but part of the family were also merchants in Markinch listed as selling china, stoneware and rags.

Helen moved to Kingskettle with David where they had seven children; William Petrie (1833-1906), Helen Petrie (1835-), John Petrie (1837-1918), Margaret Petrie (1839-), Andrew Petrie (1844-1912), my great grandfather, and David Barlas Petrie (1850-1907).

In 1822, David along with his brother James and his wife Mary went to Edinburgh to participate in the first visit to Scotland by a reigning monarch (George IV) in nearly two

The Fife Stagecoach

centuries. They travelled by stagecoach from Kingskettle to Falkland, then Markinch, then Dunfermline and onto North Queensferry where they took a newly launched steam ferry, Queen Margaret across the Firth of Forth to South Queensferry. The 40-mile-long trip took a day and a half with a probable overnight stay in Dunfermline. Their next overnight stay was in South Queensferry at the Queensferry Arms. From there they would have either walked or taken a local stagecoach to central Edinburgh to see the king. It seems like an arduous journey but if you have ever seen a Jane Austen (1775-1817) period film you will see that stagecoach travel was quite common if you didn't own your own horse and carriage. Travelling this way wasn't cheap but a trip to see the king, I imagine, was a special, once in a lifetime occasion.

Now, why would they have undertaken this journey that undoubtedly was a wee bit dear for them. The entire royal visit was orchestrated by Sir Walter Scott who in 1817 had published his romantic account of Rob Roy MacGregor. Remember our MacGregor connection. He was helped in managing the pageantry of the event by another MacGregor, William Henry Murray who had published advertisements in local newspapers appealing to MacGregors to lend their support to the visit and demonstrate the newly found importance of the MacGregor clan. David Petrie and family, being of an adventurous nature took up the offer, perhaps not out of loyalty to the monarch but to enjoy the spectacle and excess of the English king.

George IV

The portly king, known for his love of fashion and frippery, dressed to impress in full highland regalia, kilt and all. Apparently, his outfit cost 1,355 pounds, equivalent to 120,000 pounds today. Unfortunately, the king's pride caused the wrong measurements to be given to the tailor and the kilt was too short, finishing well above the knees. Rather than risk showing his bare legs and other parts, he wore pink tights. He only appeared once in full highland dress wearing the kilt, but it has remained as the enduring image of the visit to this day.

The kilt had been prohibited by the Dress Act (repealed in 1782) as part of the punishment on highlanders for their part in the Jacobite uprising of 1745, although it was still used by Scots serving in the English army. Sir Walter Scott's instructions for the Highland Ball, a highlight of the visit was for gentlemen, if not in uniform, must wear the ancient highland costume. This was the start of a rebirth in the wearing of a kilt for special occasions, establishing it as the national dress, pardon the pun, of Scotland.

The royal visit lasted 20 days starting on August 12. The festivities featured parades, levees, concerts and appearances by the royal personage. On August 20th a levee was held at Holyrood House for the high and mighty of Edinburgh. It was attended by 457 ladies each of whom the king insisted on kissing. The king in addition to his obesity was known for his halitosis or bad breath. Shortly after the levee ended the nursery rhyme, "Georgie Porgy, pudding and pie, kissed the girls and made them cry" could be heard echoing the streets of Edinburgh, or so the story goes. I'm sure the Petries added to the mirth.

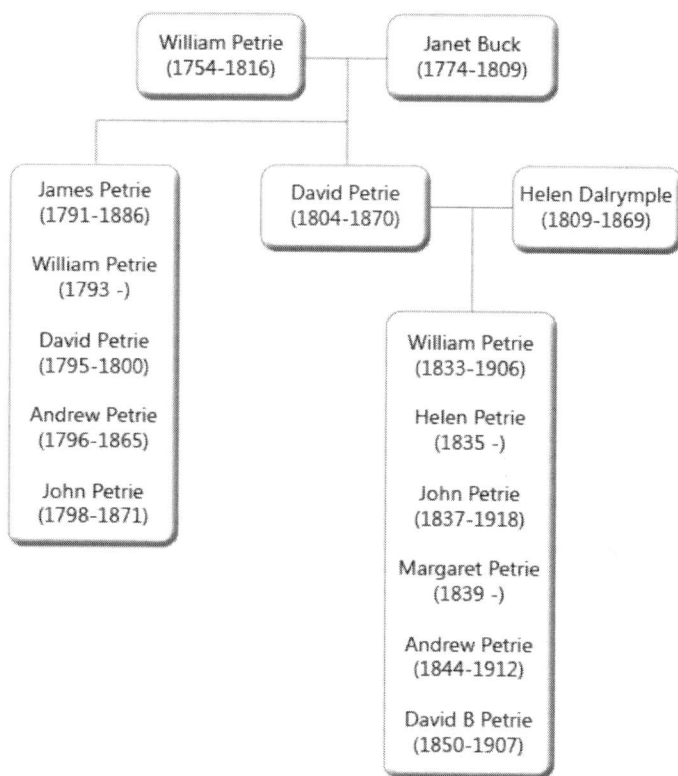

| William Petrie (1754-1816) | Janet Buck (1774-1809) |

| James Petrie (1791-1886) | David Petrie (1804-1870) | Helen Dalrymple (1809-1869) |

William Petrie
(1793 -)

David Petrie
(1795-1800)

Andrew Petrie
(1796-1865)

John Petrie
(1798-1871)

William Petrie
(1833-1906)

Helen Petrie
(1835 -)

John Petrie
(1837-1918)

Margaret Petrie
(1839 -)

Andrew Petrie
(1844-1912)

David B Petrie
(1850-1907)

EPISODE 10

DAVID PETRIE & HELEN DALRYMPLE

David and Helen Petrie's children were all born in Kingskettle and all except for my great-grandfather Andrew lived and died within the parish of Kettle.

Their eldest son, William Petrie (1833-1906) worked as a linen weaver, helping his father until he was 30 and then he and his wife, Marion Fyfe moved to the coal mining village of Cowdenbeath, Fife where he became a miner. William must not have been able to keep much of the coal he mined, so he found other ways to stay warm at night. They had 12 children. Three moved to New Zealand and two to Canada.

Janet Petrie (1842-1907) lived with her parents at Bankton Park and worked as a cook. After the death of her parents in 1869 and 1870 she appears to have had a daughter, Jessie (1869-1893) though there is no record of a marriage or birth. At some point, she and her daughter moved in to take care of her sister Helen who by then was an invalid.

Helen Petrie (1883-1910) and William Melville (1837-) had one son, James Petrie Melville born in 1854, and ten grandchildren. Several of the grandchildren immigrated to Canada and one to California. I'm not sure if Helen and William were married or not but, in the census of 1861, Helen is listed as living at home with her parents and young son, James. There is no further mention of William Melville.

Margaret Louisa Petrie (1839-1912) married Robert Arnott from Falkland, Fife. They had five children together. Margaret had another child before marrying Robert. They all lived in Kettle for most of their lives.

Lindores House

Lady Catherine Maitland

John Petrie (1837-1918) left home at the age of 12 and went to work as a companion/house servant for Lady Catherine Maitland of Lindores House, a few miles west of Kettle. Lady Catherine was the wife of British Admiral Sir Frederick Lewis Maitland, a hero of the Napoleonic wars. The couple had one male child who died in infancy. Lady Catherine, apparently wanted the company of a young boy around the house after her husband died at sea. A portrait of Lady Catherine by Sir Henry Raeburn currently hangs in the Metropolitan Museum of Art in New York.

John married Betsy Ogg Hutton and they had eight children, 15 great-grandchildren, some of who immigrated to the United States and many great-great-grandchildren. After leaving Lindores House, John worked as a woodcutter for a few years and eventually went to work for the Edinburgh and Northern Railway in Ladybank, Fife. I came across an old newspaper clipping from Methilhill about John.

"With shock last week did we notice that the picturesque little cottage at Pirnie Level Crossing was earmarked for demolition.

Natives of this district at home and abroad will think with a pang of regret that not only have honest old John Petrie and his dear wife, Betsy gone from our midst but that soon even the home of which they were so proud – a source of delight to everyone passing – is soon to be a place of the past. Full of years, Mr. Petrie died some eight winters ago (1918). His partner and helpmate for over 30 years bore up wonderfully in her loneliness, but when winter set in it was deemed better that at her great age, Granny – she – was 92 – should reside with her family in Kinghorn. There she passed away peacefully. Their life was an epic of honoured independence and industry."

Not long after their wedding, John employed in the railway goods yard at Ladybank, fell across the rails in front of a train, which deprived him of his right arm and left hand. Crippled thus cruelly, he did not despair, the couple were posted to the level-crossing, and John, with the ingenuity born of necessity, devised ways and means of doing many manual acts. He loved his garden, he kept it spotless and thrice did win the prize for the best-kept garden. With his poultry and pig and gates to attend, he had a busy life, and died at a ripe old age."

David Barlas Petrie (1850-1907) was the youngest of David and Helen's children. He married Margaret Lockhart from Dairsie, Fife and they lived in Kingskettle. They had 11 children. David worked as a maltman in a brewery for a few years and then in the Beveridge Arthurfield Works linen factory in Kingskettle for the rest of his career. Several direct descendants of David and Helen live in Kettle to this day.

Andrew Petrie (1844-1912) and Barbara Swan (1847-1920) are my great-grandparents. They were married in 1867 in Freuchie, Fife and had nine children; David Petrie (1868-1941), William Petrie (1871-), Andrew Petrie (1837-1952), Robert Petrie (1875-1878), Janet Ness Petrie (1877-1949), Helen Dalrymple Petrie (1878-), Alexandrina Swan Petrie (1881-1920), John Petrie (1882-1941), my grandfather, and Edward Swan (1885-).

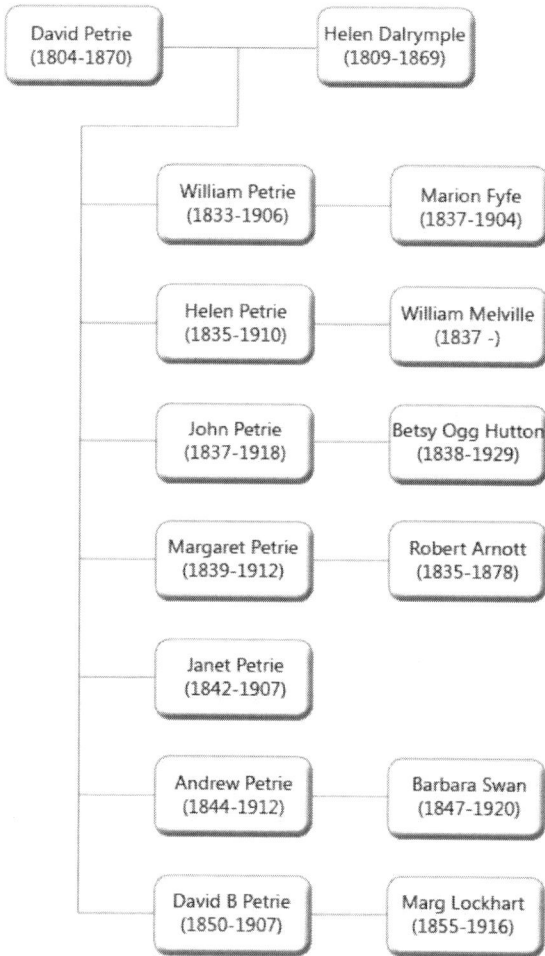

EPISODE 11

THE OTHER PETRIES

There was another family of Petries living in Kingskettle at the same time as my grandparents David Petrie and Helen Dalrymple.

Andrew Petrie

In 1831, Andrew Petrie (1798-1872) moved to New South Wales in Australia with his family aboard the Paddle Wheeler, James Watt. Andrew was an architect and builder having apprenticed with prominent Scottish architect, Alexander Lang in Edinburgh. After early success in designing several public buildings in Sydney, Andrew was put in charge of building penal colony facilities at Goat Island and Moreton Bay, which became Brisbane. The Petrie family were the first non-convict settlers to settle in the area and built a stone house on what is now known as "Petrie

Bight". He eventually established his own building firm in Brisbane and was responsible for building many of the government and other prominent buildings in Brisbane, many of which still stand.

The Petries had nine sons and one daughter. His eldest son, John eventually took over the family business and became the first Mayor of Brisbane. Another son, Thomas became an expert in aboriginal tribes, their customs and language and a leading humanitarian in Queensland. The town of Petrie, just outside Brisbane is named after him. Today there are thousands of Petries living in this part of Australia, direct descendants of Andrew Petrie.

Andrew Petrie Residence, Brisbane

Now, why is all of this of interest? Andrew Petrie was born in Kingskettle. His parents Walter Petrie and Margaret Hutchinson were also born in Kingskettle but Walter's family came from Monikie, Angus. These Petries arrived in Kettle from Monikie around the same time as my great grandparents and were also employed in the linen weaving trade. Andrew Petrie's family, before he moved to Edinburgh lived one block from my Petries. At the time Kingskettle was a small village, so the two Petrie families must have known each other especially with such similar backgrounds. The only thing I cannot prove is a direct genetic relation. But I'm sure it is there somewhere.

CHAPTER TWO

THE MODERN PETRIES

EPISODE 12

ANDREW PETRIE & BARBARA SWAN

The story of the modern Petries starts with my great-grandparents, Andrew Petrie and Barbara Swan. Andrew was born on January 15, 1844, at number 7 Bankton Park, Kettle, Fife. His father still operated the handloom, weaving linen at home, but the call for home-woven material was declining in favour of machine-produced products coming from the newly opened mills. Many experienced weavers including many Petries moved from their cottage looms to the mills for better pay. Andrew's older brother, William was the only sibling to continue working at home on the loom.

At the age of 16, Andrew left home to work as a ploughman on the Easter Lothrick Farm in Fife. In 1866, he met Barbara Swan from Freuchie, Fife, a small village about three miles south of Kingskettle. The Swan family were also linen weavers and had lived in Freuchie for several generations. Andrew and Barbara were married on December 20, 1867, in Freuchie and moved in with Barbara's parents.

My father and his brothers used to joke that "We (Petries) are the way we are because we are from a place called Freaky". Well actually, it's Freuchie pronounced *FRU KEY*. Freuchie is an

ancient village in Fife, at the foot of the Lomond Hills in the parish of Falkland. Located two miles east of the town of Falkland and three miles south of Kingskettle, Freuchie is described as a quaint old place with narrow winding streets and small cobble-paved courtyards. It has not changed much since the times when people travelled on foot or horseback and goods were transported by pack-horses. During the time when Falkland Palace was the home to Scotland's monarchs, Freuchie was the place where disgraced courtiers were sent to await execution. Hence an old proverbial saying in the area, "Awa tae Freuchie an eat mice" By 1867, Freuchie had a population of 965, a power loom factory, a hotel and two Presbyterian churches.

Fife Coal Miners 1900

In 1868, Andrew and Barbara moved to Markinch, Fife where Andrew got a job as a coal miner in the coal mines at Coull about a mile from where they lived. In June of 1868 their first child, David was born in Markinch.

In 1870, they moved to the mining town of Carnwath which is about 30 miles south of Edinburgh in Lanarkshire where Andrew continued to work as a coal miner. A year later their second child, William was born. Andrew, Barbara and the two children spent Christmas 1872 with Barbara's parents in

Freuchie and decided to move back to Freuchie. The move happened a week later and on January 20, 1873, their son Andrew Jr. was born. Andrew secured a job as a coal salesman and they rented a stone cottage on Church Street in Freuchie.

In 1875, son Robert was born and in 1877 their first daughter Janet Ness was born. Sadly, in March 1878 Robert died of consumption which probably means he

Church Street, Freuchie

had pulmonary tuberculosis. But later that year another daughter, Helen Dalrymple, known as Nellie was born. The next year, 1882 my grandfather, John was born.

In 1885, Barbara's sister Helen gave birth to a son, Edward Guthrie Swan, Helen was unmarried at the time so it was decided that the baby would be raised by Barbara and Andrew. By 1901 Edward had become Edward Guthrie Petrie although no formal adoption is registered. He did change his name back to Swan later in life.

EPISODE 13

~⚜P⚜~

THOSE WHO LEFT

T he turn of the century brought great change to Scotland. Some folks prospered and others toiled at underpaid and often dangerous jobs. The years between 1890 and 1920 saw many waves of emigration from Scotland to other parts of the British Empire and the United States.

David Petrie and Helen Dalrymple had seven children, one immigrated to Canada (Andrew Petrie) which I will talk about in the next episode while two others had children who also left Scotland (William Petrie and John Petrie). This is a bit of their story.

William Petrie and Marion Fyfe

William Petrie, David and Helen's oldest son and his wife Marion Fyfe had 12 children, five of whom decided to leave Scotland. All of William and Marion's family worked in coal mining. The boys worked underground, the girls worked above ground at the pithead and one tended to the pit ponies. It was dirty and dangerous work but was the lifeblood of

44

Petrie Coal Miners

many communities across Scotland for generations with Fife being a main coal mining area for hundreds of years. The industrial revolution increased the demand for coal and Fife's easy access to ports made coal mining a sought-after occupation, even if one's chances of being injured or killed were over 50 percent. Escaping this sort of life was the motivation for five of William and Marion's children to emigrate.

The first to leave was Robert Fyfe Petrie who through a promotion by the Canadian Pacific Railroad was given ranch land in Elcan, Alberta, Canada. He was joined by his wife Annie McNab (1872-1954) in 1904 and their children: Marion Fyfe Petrie (1894-1973) who married William Cornwell; Allison Martin Petrie (1895-1943) who married Sam Viter; William Petrie (1898-1993) who married Clara Louise Brodie; and Annie McNab Petrie (1902-1993) who married Herbert Matthews. In Canada, they had three more children: Duncan Petrie (1905-1906); Donald McNab Petrie (1909-1995) who married May Davey; and David Alexander Petrie (1913-1980) who married Elvira Millard.

Robert Fyfe Petrie

Annie McNab

Robert and Annie had ten great-grandchildren who settled in British Columbia, Ontario, Alberta and New York.

In 1905, Janet Petrie, granddaughter of William and Marion, and her husband James Hunter left for Canada. They settled in Hamilton, Ontario. They had three children: Robert Hunter (1904-1969) who married Bessie Olive Dolan; Reita May Hunter (1909-1997) who married Harold Morrison; and Lillian Alexander Jeanette Hunter (1911-2005) who married John Duncan Willson. All of their children lived in Hamilton or Burlington, Ontario. They had no great-grandchildren.

David Petrie, son of William and Marion married Helen Fox (1857-1941) in 1879. They had ten children: Christina Petrie (1880-1928) who married John Melville; William Petrie (1882-1932) who married Maude Zealandia Rush; Francis Petrie (1885-1961) who married Harriet Cato Allen; Janet Petrie (1886-1966) who married Frederick Fox; Marion Violet Petrie (1888-1966) who married Andrew Chapman; David Petrie (1890-1974); James Petrie (1895-1916); Annie Petrie (1896-1990) who married Thomas Mosley; Robert Petrie (1898-); and John Petrie (1899-1901). All were born in Scotland where their father worked as a coal miner.

In November 1905, David Petrie left for New Zealand on the ship, S.S. Ayrshire along with all of his sons. A year later Helen followed with the remaining family sailing on the S.S. Dorset. David died in 1931 in Dunedin, New Zealand. Helen died ten years later again in Dunedin. David and Helen had five great-grandchildren that I know of. However, I have met online, Gavin Petrie who is the grandson of William and Maude Petrie.

Alexander, known as Sandy Petrie (another son of William and Marion Petrie), was a coal miner for the first 20 odd years of his working life in Scotland. In 1883 he married Mary McDonald from Lochgelly, Fife. They had three children: a daughter Janet Given Petrie (1884-1982) who married James Hunter; a son William Petrie (1887-1977) who married

Minetta Gertrude Price; and another daughter, Mary Grace Fyfe Petrie (1895-1986) who married William John Smyth.

In 1905, Sandy and Mary's daughter, Janet Hunter immigrated to Hamilton, Ontario, Canada. Shortly after arriving Janet wrote home to her parents announcing that Canada was a wonderful place to live and jobs were plentiful in the Hamilton area. So, on December 8, 1906, Sandy, Mary and their two remaining children arrived in St. John, New Brunswick, Canada, aboard the S.S. Empress of Britain. By early 1907, they had made their way to Hamilton and moved in with Janet and her husband.

Sandy Petrie   Mary McDonald

Sandy died in 1938 and Mary a year later in 1939. They had ten great-grandchildren who settled in Hamilton, Campbellford and Ottawa, Ontario.

William Petrie, another son of William and Marion was also a coal miner in Scotland. In 1888, he married Ann Fox (1864-1960) from Ballingry, Fife. They had five children: Andrew Fox Petrie (1889-1946) who married Daisy Ruth Wilson; David Petrie (1892-1974) who married Alice Vera Milnes; James Petrie (1893-); Christina Petrie (1897-1985) who married Rowland Eyre Hayward; and William Petrie (1898-1965) who married Hilda Fanny Collins.

In 1908, after hearing from his brother David, William and his entire family immigrated to Otago, New Zealand. From this point, records are a bit sketchy but I do know there were grandchildren all of whom lived or still live in New Zealand.

John Petrie and Betsy Ogg Hutton

John Petrie and Betsy Ogg Hutton's, daughter Helen (Nellie) Petrie (1867-1948) was married to Andrew Campbell (1863-1927) and they lived in Kingskettle, Fife. They had six children. All but one, Maggie decided to immigrate to the United States along with their families. The first to move was Bessie (1890-1978) who was married to Alexander Daries (1887-1971). After a short stay in New York in 1912, they settled in Hempstead, Nassau County, just outside New York City.

They were followed in 1922 by Peter Petrie Campbell (1893-1970) and his wife Agnes Brown (1898 -); Andrew Campbell (1907-2006) and his wife Margaret White (1913-2006); and John Petrie Campbell 91897-1982) and his wife Margaret (1896 -). They also settled in Hempstead. In 1930, Jessie Petrie Campbell (1899-1978) and her husband Alex Gordon (1897-1970) also moved to Hempstead, New York.

Nellie Campbell's (Petrie), husband Andrew died in 1927 in Kettle, Fife. Shortly thereafter, she left for the United States and moved in with her son Peter in Hempstead where she died in 1948.

Nellie Campbell

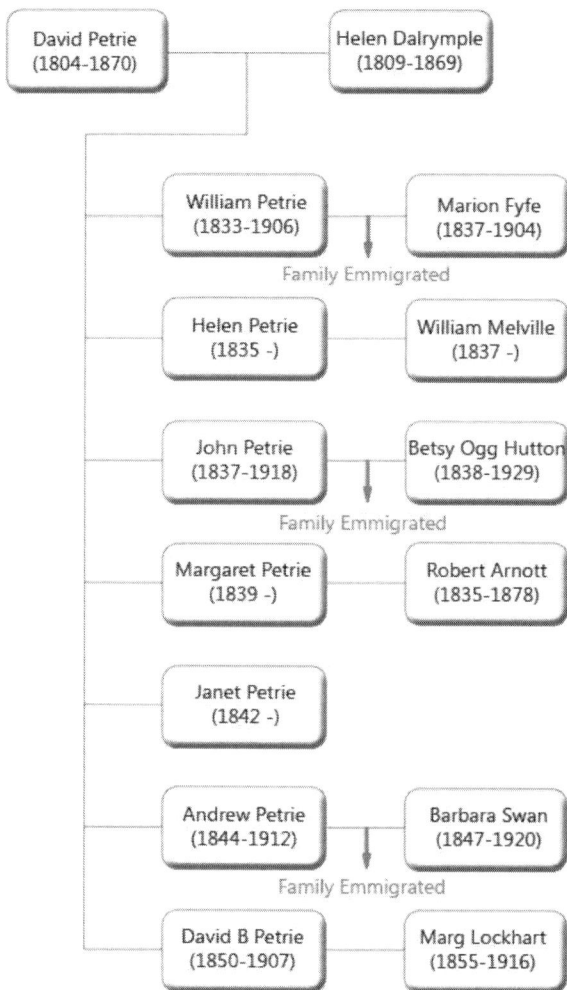

EPISODE 14

⤜⟐P⟐⤛

ANDREW & BARBARA'S BIG MOVE

In 1890, Andrew Petrie and his family moved to Dundee where Andrew got a job working as a labourer for Alexander Thomson & Sons, Verdant Works jute mill. Verdant Works was the largest jute and linen mill in Scotland. It started in 1790 and by the time Andrew went to work for them, it had moved much of its business to India using

Verdant Works Mill, Dundee

machinery and workers from Dundee. They still had over 500 employees in Dundee including many women and children under the age of 14. Every member of the family except for Barbara got jobs working in the mill - even the younger ones who were in their early teens. The family lived in a rented house at 9 Tannadice Street in Dundee and by 1901 had moved to a larger house at 9 Roslin

Terrace, Dundee. At the age of 57, Andrew had become a foreman at the jute mill.

When Andrew first started working in the Dundee jute mill, its' glory days had already passed with much of the factory being used to re-cycle jute waste products as well as cure rabbit skins and store scrap metal. By 1902, Andrew could see that his future in the mill was limited. His boss, Mr. Menzie told him that because of his age, his prospects were not good and he should start thinking about retiring. The future also looked uncertain for Andrew's children at the mill. It was time for a change, but to what?

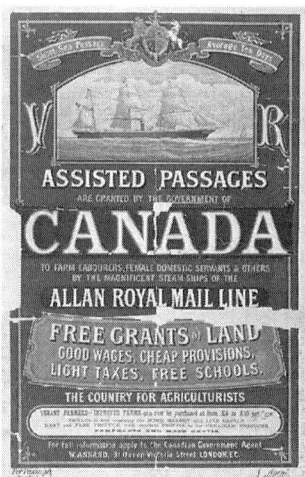

Sometime during 1902, Andrew had a letter from his older brother William about William's son Robert who had just immigrated to Canada and had been given a land grant in Saskatchewan. The letter said that Robert was singing the praises of Canada, "a land of opportunities for all". During the same time, the Government of Canada was actively promoting Scottish emigrants to settle in Canada, especially to western provinces. It set up recruitment offices in most major centres in Scotland. Agents travelled the country, pasting up posters, giving lectures, handing out pamphlets and trying one-by-one to persuade farmers and labourers of the virtues of life in Canada. Similar efforts were being made by other British colonies: notably New Zealand, Australia and South Africa. The son of a neighbour had recently immigrated to Toronto and wrote to his parents that Toronto was full of Scots especially in the police force, fire department and skilled labour jobs.

Over Christmas 1902, son Andrew, 29 at the time announced that he was going to immigrate to either Canada or the United States. He saw no future for him in Dundee or anywhere else in Scotland and thought the rest of the family should join him. This started a discussion that lasted many days until, in early January it was decided that the entire family except for the eldest son David would pool their savings, pack up and leave for Canada. Montreal was selected as their first stop but they were thinking of Toronto or western Canada as a possible final destination. Back then immigration to Canada from Scotland was a relatively easy thing. Canada at the time was still a colony and all Canadians were British subjects. Therefore, moving to Canada was not much different than moving to another part of Britain. Canada at the time was looking for skilled labour as immigrants so Andrew was listed on the ship's manifest as a fireman. Although I cannot find any record of him ever being a fireman in Scotland.

Sons William and Andrew along with Janet's husband WilliamMcGuigan were sent ahead of the rest of the family to scout potential work and lodging for the family. They

S.S. Corinthian

sailed in late October 1903 on the S.S. Corinthian for Montreal and eventually ended up in Toronto by mid-November of that year.

After hearing back from William and the boys that prospects looked good for a future life in Toronto, the passage was booked on the S.S. Buenos Ayrean in second class for April 30, 1904, for Andrew, Barbara, Nellie, Alexandrina, John Hoskins her fiancé and Janet (McGuigan) and her children, Arthur and Helen. John and his uncle, James Swan travelled in steerage class. The ship was bound for Quebec City and Montreal in Canada.

EPISODE 15

※ P ※

THE VOYAGE

The S.S. Buenos Ayrean was owned by the Allan Line, a Scottish-Canadian shipping company founded by Captain Alexander Allan in 1819. Allan's two sons established offices in

S.S. Buenos Ayrean

Greenock (Glasgow), Liverpool and Montreal and in 1856 was a dominant player in Scotland to Montreal shipping routes. With innovative designs and engineering, the Allan line prospered on the Atlantic and other routes. The first steel liner to sail the Atlantic was the Buenos Ayrean, launched in 1880. The ship was 4,005 tons, 385' long with a width of 42'. It had a single propeller and could muster a top speed of 12 knots. It was scrapped in 1911. On my relatives' voyage, the Ship's Master was Captain B.T. Eastaway. After the turn of the century, the Allan Line had difficulty financing new ships and was sold to Canadian Pacific Steamships Ltd. in 1909.

Two days before their scheduled departure, with all their worldly belongings packed, the Petries took the train to Glasgow. According to Barbara's diary, April 30th was a dull and rainy day as they sailed from Greenock down the Clyde towards the Irish Sea and out into the Atlantic. The weather never improved and several days out almost everyone became seasick. Those in second class were allowed on the outer decks to get some relief, but John and James in steerage weren't so lucky.

Barbara described their cabin as quite comfortable with running water and close access to the WC. The meals, when they could eat were "substantial and more than adequate". I discovered a second-class menu from their trip for Sunday, May 1, 1904.

Breakfast A choice of:	Luncheon A choice of:	Dinner A choice of:
Strawberries Oatmeal porridge Fried Plaice Grilled Ham Fried eggs Broiled sausage Curried chicken and rice Dry hash	Barley broth Beef Steak Pie Corned Beef and vegetables Cold boiled beef Baked potato, Boiled rice Sage pudding, Peach tart Cheese and crackers	Spring soup Broiled cod with parsley sauce Stewed rabbit Roast beef and Yorkshire pudding Roast turkey and cranberry sauce Oxtongue Baked potatoes, cauliflower Plum pudding, Apple tart, ice cream Cheese and crackers

Sounds not too bad. I wonder what was served in steerage.

Allan Line Docks, Montreal

On May 13, 1904, they landed in Montreal and the sun was shining. From Montreal, they took the train to Toronto and were met at Union Station by William Petrie, Andrew Petrie and William McGuigan. A month before their arrival much of the downtown area of Toronto had been destroyed by fire. The boys announced that there was work for everyone helping to rebuild the city. There was also an abundance of rooming houses and private homes looking for lodgers so immediate accommodation was not a problem.

Old Union Station, Toronto

EPISODE 16

PEARS AVENUE

In 1905, a year after arriving in Toronto, Andrew Petrie and William McGuigan bought a plot of land on Pears Avenue in Toronto's Yorkville neighbourhood. In 1851, Leonard Pears (cousin of the founder of the Pears Soap Company in England) opened a brickwork just west of Yonge Street and north of Belmont Street. Known as the Yorkville Brick Yards, it employed 60 men and produced six million bricks a year. The unique clay in the area produced a yellowish-white brick that was highly sought after. These bricks were used to build many prominent buildings in Toronto that still stand today including St. Lawrence Hall, St. James Cathedral and St. Michael's Cathedral. Mr. Pears retired in 1889 and the brickworks was closed in 1904 and turned into a park.

The Pears family called their home "Summerhill" on Avenue Road, just west of the brickworks. They opened a road from the brickyard to the house, paved with yellow bricks (the original yellow brick road) that was to become Pears Avenue.

Pears Avenue by Albert Franck

My great-grandfather, Andrew and his son-in-law, William bought a set of plans for a "prefab house" in the Edwardian style popular in Toronto at the time. The term prefab meant that lumber, doors, windows etc. for the house were pre-cut or manufactured by a local lumber merchant. Between all the Petrie clan they had enough talent and expertise to build the house which was actually two semi-detached buildings. Construction took a little over a year and by summer 1906 numbers 57 and 59 Pears Avenue were ready to be occupied.

The design for 57/59 Pears Avenue was typical for the time and featured a front gable window, generous front porch and brick exterior. Inside was a central hallway that went from the front door to the kitchen in the back. On one side, were

Typical Edwardian House 1910

doors to a living room and a dining room. I recall these rooms were divided by heavy velvet curtains. On the other side of the hall was the staircase upstairs with the stairs to the

Andrew Petrie

basement located below. The second floor had three bedrooms and a bathroom. The front bedroom was the master with a generous window. The house initially

Barbara Swan

57

had gas lighting which was the least expensive option for the time. This was later (1920) converted to electricity with the wiring being fed through the old gas lines. The basement had an enormous coal-fired, gravity urnace with a large coal bin. The furnace was not converted to oil until the late 1950s. A driveway down one side of the house led to a two-storey garage in the back yard.

Andrew and Barbara, their daughter, Alexandrina and sons William and John moved into number 59 and William McGuigan, his wife Janet (Petrie) and their children Arthur, Helen and May moved into number 57.

After 68 years of hard work, Andrew died on March 28, 1912. Barbara died at the age of 73 on November 12, 1920. They are both buried in the family plot in Mount Pleasant Cemetery in Toronto.

EPISODE 17

GREAT UNCLES & AUNTS

This is the story of my great uncles and aunts who immigrated to Canada in 1904. The only ones not mentioned are my grand-parents, John Petrie and Margaret Owens whom I talk about in a subsequent episode.

William Petrie

Andrew and Barbara's son, William Petrie while helping to build the house at 59 Pears Avenue started to work for the Toronto Transit Commission in 1906. By 1911, he was working full time as a streetcar conductor with an annual salary of $572. In August 1912, he married Christine Dawson a fellow Scot who had arrived in Canada in 1905. They lived at 59 Pears Avenue until 1914 when they bought a

TTC Streetcar 1906

house at 326 Howland Avenue, just across the road from his

sister Nellie and her husband Sam Reid. In 1914, William left the T.T.C., and worked until his retirement in 1951, as the caretaker for the Ontario Parliament Buildings. He died a year later. William and Christine had two daughters, Jean and Anna. Christine continued to live at 326 Howland Avenue until 1957 after which she moved into a nursing home in Swansea (part of Toronto).

Andrew Petrie Jr.

Just after the houses at 57/59 Pears Avenue were finished Andrew Jr. was married. On August 15, 1906, he married his first cousin Janet Ness Swan, daughter of William Swan (Barbara's niece) and Isabella Law. The wedding reception was held at Pears Avenue. A few months later the couple moved to Plainfield, New Jersey, USA where Andrew got a job as a machinist with the Walter Scot Company. They lived at 142 Jackson Avenue in Plainfield until 1919 when they moved back to Scotland, first to Freuchie, Fife and then to Monifieth in Angus. Janet died in 1951 followed by Andrew a year later on September 30, 1952. Andrew's obituary read *"Mr. Andrew Petrie (79) of 11A High Street, Monifieth was found dead in his home yesterday. Retired, he lived alone and is believed to have been last seen at a local football match on Saturday. The cause of death was thrombosis, hypertension."*

Andrew and Janet had no family. I did hear gossip that it was because they were first cousins.

Janet Ness Petrie

Janet Ness Petrie was the oldest daughter of Andrew and Barbara Petrie. She worked alongside her father and brothers in the Alexander Thomson & Sons jute mill in Dundee from an early age until she married William McGuigan on December 1, 1899, in Dundee. McGuigan was from Ballyclare, Northern Ireland and had been working in the

Dundee jute mill for several years. Janet and William had two children, Arthur Green McGuigan (1900-1964) and Helen McGuigan (1903-1980).

In 1903, William journeyed to Canada with his brothers-in-law William and Andrew Petrie to look at immigration prospects for the Petrie family. In 1904, Janet accompanied by her parents and siblings joined William in Toronto. They helped Janet's father; Andrew build their future home at 57 Pears Avenue. In 1905, another daughter, Mary (May) McGuigan (1905-1990) was born and in 1908 another son was born, Andrew Petrie (1908-1909) who sadly died a year later. William worked as a factory labourer. He and Janet lived at 57 Pears Avenue until 1932 when the family moved to Oakland, California.

By 1935 William and Janet had moved to Stanislaus, California to live on a farm with their daughter Helen and her husband Hardy Erickson. Just after the United States entered World War II, they moved back to Oakland where William went to work in a war production plant. In 1949, Janet died and was followed by William in 1953.

Helen Dalrymple Petrie

Helen Dalrymple Petrie, known as Nellie, like the rest of her family, worked in the Alexander Thomson & Sons jute mill in Dundee from the age of 12 until her family immigrated to Canada in 1904. Nellie lived with her parents at 59 Pears Avenue until 1907 when she married Sam Reid who was living at the time at 93 Pears Avenue. Sam was a bricklayer and had immigrated to Canada in 1904 as well. The couple lived at 93 Pears Avenue until 1911 when they bought a house at 329 Howland Avenue in Toronto. Nellie's brother William was to buy a house across the road from them a few years later.

Nellie and Sam had four children: Robert Templeton Reid (1908-); Andrew Petrie Reid (1911-); Barbara Reid (1912-); and Jean Reid (1919-)

Sam served with the British Army in South Africa during the Boer War and was awarded the Distinguished Conduct Medal. He also enlisted with the Canadian Over-Seas Expeditionary Force in World War I from 1914 to 1918 and was awarded the Military Medal for Bravery.

Distinguished Conduct Medal

The Reids lived at 329 Howland until 1925 when they moved to 1520 Ossington Avenue, Toronto. From this point sadly I cannot find any further information about the family.

Alexandrina Petrie

Andrew and Barbara's daughter, Alexandrina, like her parents and siblings worked in the Dundee jute mill. In 1901, she was listed as a jute yarn winder. It was at the mill in 1900 she met John Hoskins from Dundee. Hoskins's family was from Montrose, Angus, Scotland.

When the Petries decided to immigrate to Canada in 1904, John Hoskins contributed his savings and came with them. He was listed at the time as Alexandrina's fiancé. They were married on September 15, 1911, and my grandparents, John Petrie and Margaret Owens were witnesses. At the time, John was a professional chauffeur for the Imperial Motor Car Company. They lived at 59 Pears Avenue with Alexandrina's parents until 1920. On August 1, 1912, Alexandrina gave birth to a daughter, Barbara Swan Hoskins.

On August 24, 1920, Alexandrina died while giving birth to a premature baby, who also did not survive. Alexandrina is buried along with her parents in the Petrie family plot in Mount Pleasant Cemetery in Toronto.

John Hoskins subsequently moved to 915 Woodbine Avenue in Toronto and in 1924 married Margaret Campbell. He died in 1953 while at home at his Woodbine Avenue home.

Edward Swan

Edward Guthrie Swan/Petrie moved to Toronto in 1905 and rented a house at 50 Pears Avenue. By 1911, he had married Christina (last name unknown) and was still living on Pears Avenue. In 1915 he joined the Canadian Over-Seas Expeditionary Force. It is not clear if he actually served overseas. Christina died in 1920 and was buried in a single plot in Toronto's Prospect Cemetery. Her listed address at the time was 68 Boon Avenue, Toronto. From this point on there are no further records of Edward.

The Petries in front of 57/59 Pears Avenue.
Front row left to right: William McGuigan; Janet Ness Petrie (McGuigan); Arthur Green McGuigan; Andrew Petrie; Barbara Swan (Petrie); Margaret Owens (Petrie); John Petrie Back row left to right: Sam Reid; Helen Dalrymple Petrie (Reid); Barbara Reid; Andrew Petrie Jr.; Janet Ness Swan (Petrie)

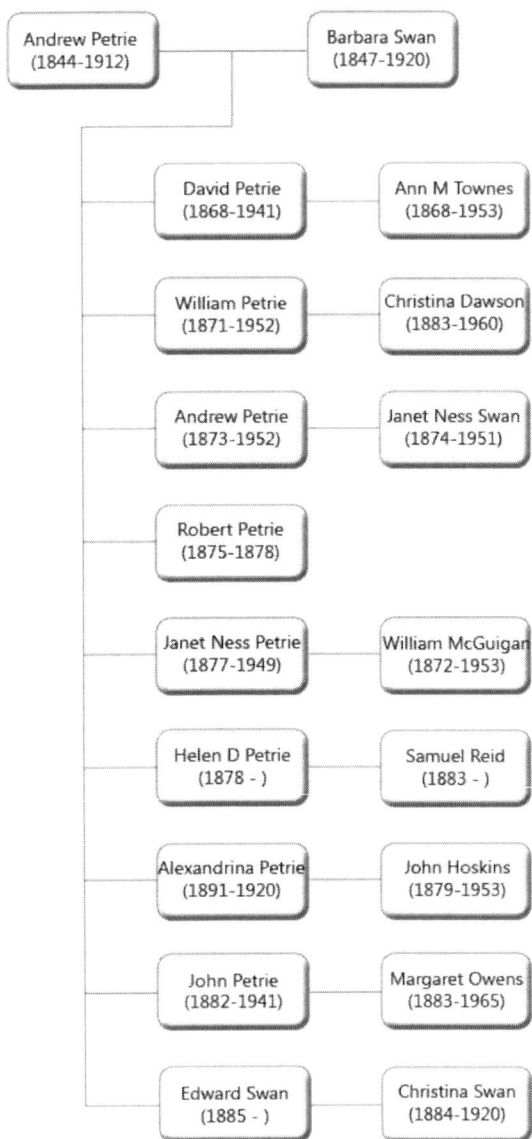

EPISODE 18

JOHN & MARGARET PETRIE

My grandfather, John Petrie was listed in the 1901 Scotland census, at the age of 18 as an apprentice mechanic at the Dundee jute mill where his parents and siblings also worked. He sailed with his family to Canada in 1904 but travelled in steerage class on the S.S. Buenos Ayrean with his uncle James Swan.

John helped his father and brother-in-law William McGuigan build their house at 59 Pears Avenue where he lived for the rest of his life. In 1911, at the age of 28 his parents and siblings, William and Alexandrina also lived at 59 Pears Avenue. At that point, John was working as an auto mechanic earning an annual salary of $675.

Andrew Owens

On August 31, 1912, just a few months after the death of his father, in a civil ceremony, John married his long-time girlfriend, Margaret Owens. Margaret was born in Rutherglen (Glasgow), Scotland in 1883 and immigrated to Toronto in 1908 with her family, Andrew Owens (1859-1944) and Elizabeth Sweeney (1863-), her parents and siblings: Elizabeth Owens (1888-); Jacob Owens (1890-); John Owens (1892-1970); Isaac Owens (1895-1917); and Oliver Owens (1899-1981). The Owens family lived at 226 Soudan Avenue in Toronto.

Elizabeth Sweeney

John and Margaret had four sons: John Swan Petrie (1913-1982); and his twin Andrew Gardner Petrie (1913-1980); Francis David Petrie (1919-2005); and my father, Kenneth Owens Petrie (1923-2004).

John was encouraged by his brother-in-law, John Hoskins to become a chauffeur and worked for a while for the same car service as Hoskins, The Imperial Motor Car Company. Imperial was an early car manufacturer based in the United States with a location in Toronto. John Hoskins and John Petrie would drive cars for people who bought one of these new "horseless buggies" but were afraid to drive it themselves. The Imperial brand was eventually taken over by

Imperial Roadster
The Car with
THE STRAIGHT LINE DRIVE
50 to 55 h.p., 36-inch wheels, selective type transmission,
Eisemann magneto, double drop frame. Price, including sun
lamps and generator, horn, tools, etc., $2500.00.
Manufactured by Imperial Motor Car Company Incorporated
Main Office and Factory, Williamsport, Pa.
MEMBER A. M. C. M. A.

the Chrysler Motor Company and became the Chrysler Imperial car.

John left the company in 1914 and became an independent chauffeur, but mainly worked for the Elias Rogers Company and family. This lasted until 1923 when he joined an insurance agency called Murphy, Love, Hamilton and Bascom as a chauffeur. While working for the Rogers family, John was either given or purchased from them an oak dining room set for 59 Pears Avenue, which I now have in my home. The Rogers family were staunch Quakers as became John's family following the death of Margaret's brother Isaac Owens at Vimy Ridge during World War I.

John eventually became a clerk for Murphy, Love, Hamilton and Bascom and in 1940 joined the New York Insurance Company as an underwriter. Although times were tough, he was fortunate to be to have a job throughout the Great Depression to take care of his family. They even bought a small cottage on the Nottawasaga River north of Toronto.

John Petrie died of heart failure on December 17, 1941, and is buried in the Petrie plot along with his parents and sister in Mount Pleasant Cemetery, Toronto. Margaret was left to raise her four children on a limited pension until the boys were old enough to work and help support the household.

EPISODE 19

GRANDMA PETRIE

As a child, when I went to visit my Grandma Petrie, I was surprised at how different her house was compared to the modern suburban home we lived in. She lived at 59 Pears Avenue until she died in 1965. Her house, while tidy was filled with relics from three generations of Petries. She didn't own a television and with her brother Oliver, who now lived with her, spent evenings reading and playing cards. On one visit I was allowed to observe a meeting she was having in their front room of the local chapter of the Co-operative Commonwealth Federation (CCF), the forerunner of today's New Democratic Party. It was a small gathering as I recall with lots of arguing. My mother's family were all conservative party supporters who were appalled when I told

68

them about my grandmother's friends, "a bunch of communists".

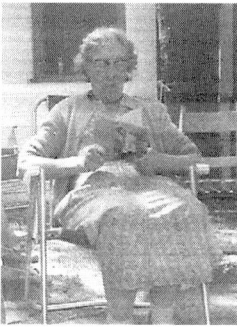

Grandma was also a Quaker, a pacifist and an ardent proponent of women's rights. Although during her early years in Scotland she was raised as a Presbyterian, her parents became members of the Society of Friends in Glasgow and brought their new beliefs to Canada when they emigrated. The Petries were Presbyterian but Margaret convinced her husband to become a Quaker after the death of her brother Isaac Owens at the Battle of Vimy Ridge. In 1918, she marched her husband and twin five-year-old sons to the Quaker Meeting House on Maitland Street in Toronto and signed them up.

Despite having limited means, her kitchen, which to me always smelled of gas, was home several times a week to many of her siblings and in-laws for lunch. I recall these old men sitting around the kitchen table eating baloney sandwiches, Bakewell tarts, drinking lemon tea and arguing about politics. During one visit, at the time of the Cuban missile crisis, my grandmother said to me that if a war came to Canada, "that evil Mr. Diefenbaker (Prime Minister of Canada at the time) will na git his hands on you laddie."

After Margaret died in August of 1965, her sons sold the house and scattered her ashes at the family cottage.

I've often wondered how much Grandma Petrie knew about the history of the Petrie family. I was a teenager when she died and of course never asked about such things. I'm sure there are many stories about my family that she didn't tell.

EPISODE 20

THEY STAYED BEHIND

The last few episodes talked about the Petries who left Scotland around the turn of the last century. There was, however, one who stayed behind. Andrew Petrie and Barbara Swan's first-born son, David decided not to immigrate to Canada with the rest of his family. David was born in 1868 in Markinch, Fife. His family had moved to Carnwath, Lanarkshire and then Freuchie, Fife. Starting at an early age in Freuchie, David had a variety of jobs to help support the family including hauling salt from the salt pans on the Fife coast and as an apprentice butcher in Freuchie. It was said that he was an enterprising young lad.

In 1890, the Petrie family moved to Dundee where most started working for the Alexander Thomson & Sons Company who owned a large jute mill in town. David started at the mill as an apprentice mechanic and eventually worked his way up to a full mechanic. At the same time, he was taking engineering courses to add to his skills.

In 1891, he married Ann McKenzie Towns who also worked at the Dundee jute mill. Ann was born in Monifieth, Angus in 1868 and moved with her family to Dundee in 1874.

When his parents and siblings decided to emigrate, David felt his prospects in Dundee were promising and did not want to move his growing family.

David and Ann had five children, all born in Dundee: Andrew Petrie (1892-1959); David Petrie (1894-1954); Isabella (Ella) Towns Petrie (1902-1985); Florence Maria Petrie (1904-1978); and Frederick Swan Petrie (1908-1977).

David continued to grow in importance at work; as a manager/engineer in Dundee and in 1921, along with his son

David Petrie

David was sent to Bombay and then Calcutta, India as a consultant to the jute industry. Many of the Dundee jute mills had relocated to India where labour was cheaper and regulations less stringent. Sound familiar? He and his son stayed in India for just under a year, returning to Dundee in 1922. He returned to India again for several months in 1932. Ann stayed in Dundee during all the India visits.

Annie Townes

In 1934, David and Ann bought an old church building in the hamlet of Johnshaven on the east coast of Aberdeenshire, just north of Montrose. They converted the church into their retirement home and lived there until David died in 1941. They also had purchased a tenement building in Dundee which provided them with rental income. Ann died at 7 Park Avenue in Dundee in 1953. All of their children remained in the Dundee area for all their lives.

EPISODE 21

⟿ P ⟾

NOTABLE PETRIES

While I may think my branch of the Petrie family is the top of the heap, so to speak, many other notable Petries may or may not be related, probably not. Here are a few that caught my eye.

Arthur Petrie, Bishop of Moray

One of Arthur's first jobs in the 1740s was as a tutor to the family Walkinshaw, not far from Glasgow, on the annual salary of six pounds per annum. Here he devoted himself so sincerely to his duties, as only a Petrie can do, that when he became ill with consumption, his family "took the most anxious care of him". Otherwise, I guess they would just have let him die.

In 1754, he wanted to immigrate to Jamaica but was persuaded to stay in Scotland by his relatives. In 1756, his mother fell ill and died. The next year he accepted a tutorship as a layman at Balgowan near Perth but stayed only a short time. In 1757, he returned to Aberdeenshire where he was put in pastoral charge of the good folks of Wartle and Meiklefolla. He was appointed the Episcopal Bishop of Moray in 1778. This was a big deal at the time.

"Tradition still relates the gratification with which Bishop Petrie was hailed when seen coming slowly up the glens on his little pony, his check plaid serving for gown and lawn sleeves."

Sounds like something from the TV series Outlander. One of his most famous actions as Bishop was the appointment and consecration of Bishop Seabury, the first Bishop of the American Episcopal Church. Bishop Petrie died in 1787 "in the fifty-sixth year of his age and the eleventh of his Episcopate."

Swedish Petries of Note

Robert Petrie, son of George Petrie the provost of Montrose, Fife, came to Sweden with his bother George soon after his father died in 1628. The route between Montrose on Scotland's east coast and Sweden was a popular trading route by the early 1600s. The Scots were adventurous people and preferred trading with Scandinavia and Europe rather than England. In Sweden, the Petrie brothers founded the Brattfors steelworks in Ockelbo. The family became one of the leading iron producers in Scandinavia. Their descendants continued to own the steelworks well into the 19th century, by which time they had diversified into hemp and jute production and were supplying jute back to Scotland for the production of linen.

Many Petrie families still live in Sweden, Norway and Denmark.

English Petries of Note

The Petres of Devon
One Petrie family had definite English origins, probably coming directly from Flemish roots. The "Petres" were yeoman farmers at Torbryan in Devon, going back to the late 1300s. John Petre was "a rich tanner of Torbryan" in the early 1500s. His son Sir John was a founding member of the "Exeter Merchant Adventurers" in the 1560s. The Merchant Adventurers were trading capitalists who rose to prominence by buying and then exporting woollen cloth from England to foreign markets, mainly in Europe. By royal charter, the Merchant Adventurers were allowed to exert control over the port of Antwerp which allowed them to enjoy an effective monopoly over the European cloth trade.

Sir William Petrie

Another son, Sir William Petre made it to London and the Tudor court, serving as Secretary of State for four monarchs from Henry VIII to Queen Elizabeth. He acquired Ingatestone Hall in Essex at the time of the dissolution of the monasteries. He established it as a Catholic refuge. It has remained under the Petre family to the present day.

The Petries of Lewisham
Another prominent family, the Petries of Lewisham in Surrey had Scottish origins. The Rev. Robert Petrie grew up on the Scottish borders and had previously been a minister in Dumfries, Scotland. He died in Lewisham in 1791.

Sir John Petrie

He had two sons who prospered in India with the East India Company before returning to England. John Petrie returned the richer of the two. He became an MP and a slave owner with plantations in the new colony of Tobago.

His brother, William Petrie had the more distinguished descendants, most notably Flinders Petrie, the father of Egyptian archaeology. Flinders was considered brilliant and the go-to person for anything to do with Egypt at the time.

Along with Lord Carnarvon (owner of Highclere Castle of Downton Abbey fame), they discovered the King Tut treasures. When Flinders died in 1942, he donated his head – and hence his brain – to the Royal College of Surgeons in London where it is now stored. The rest of his body is buried in the Protestant cemetery in Jerusalem.

Sir Flinders Petrie

Most English Petries, however, were to be found closer to Scotland, in northern England. Charles Petrie from Fife, for instance, developed his family fisheries business in Liverpool where he served as its mayor in 1901 and was made a baronet in 1918. His son, Sir Charles Petrie was a noted historian and author, his grandson Peter Petrie a British diplomat.

Sir Charles Petrie

EPISODE 22

$\sim$ P $\sim$

MORE NOTABLE PETRIES

As I said in the previous episode, while I may think my branch of the Petrie family is the top of the heap, so to speak, many other notable Petries may or may not be related, probably not. Here are a few more that caught my eye.

American Petries of note

The Petries of Herkimer County in New York were German immigrants from the Palatinate who had made their home at German Flats in the Mohawk Valley of New York in the early 1700s. The family originated in Scotland but the roots are not known. Catherine Petrie married Johan Herkimer around 1720. William Petrie was a surgeon in Nicholas Herkimer's brigade during the American Revolutionary War.

The origins of Alexander Petrie of South Carolina are uncertain. Some suspect the family originally was from New Brunswick in the British colony of Canada. Alexander was the

Alexander Petrie House

premier silversmith of Charleston from the 1740s to his death in 1768. His silver work is still highly sought after today.

American philanthropist, Milton Petrie's origins were Jewish. His parents arrived from Russia and were running a pawn shop in Salt Lake City when he was born in 1902. He made a fortune from a chain of retail stores in New Jersey, which he supplemented through canny investments in real estate and stocks. His philanthropy is

Carol & Milton Petrie Sculpture Court

displayed best in the Carroll and Milton Petrie Atrium and Terrace in New York's Metropolitan Museum of Art.

Canadian Petries of note

In Nova Scotia and Ontario, two notable Petrie British officers settled.

In Nova Scotia, George Petrie a British soldier, of Scottish descent was awarded a land grant in the 1780s because of his service to the crown. In 1789, along with his wife, Isabel he settled in Sydney on Cape Breton Island in Nova Scotia. Fort Petrie, named after them, exists there today.
Petrie descendants on Cape Breton are numerous, including the mid-19th century relatives of James Petrie at Glace Bay. His son John Petrie died on the Western Front during World War I and is recognized as a Canadian war hero.

Daniel Petrie

Daniel Petrie, born in Glace Bay in 1920, came to New York in the 1960s where he made his name as a movie and TV director. He is probably best known for directing the film "Lassie" – more Scottish connections. His family expanded there to include: two directors, Daniel Petrie and his son Donald; a television movie producer, Dorothea Petrie; a screenwriter, Dan Petrie Jr.; a movie studio executive, June Petrie and an actress, Mary Petrie.

In Ontario, another British officer from Scotland who received a Canadian land grant was Captain Archibald Petrie. He was a purser on ships patrolling Lake Ontario during the War of 1812. His land grant was in Cumberland township, Ontario where he became a prominent merchant and politician. Petrie Island on the Ottawa river is named after him.

There are many other note-worthy Petries in the world but, by now I'm sure you've had enough *Petriemania*.

CHAPTER THREE

BACK UP THE TREE

EPISODE 23

~⚜P⚜~

THE SWANS

I now want to take you up another branch of the Petrie family tree, one that I stumbled across while doing research into the villages of Freuchie and Kingskettle. My cousin, Lesley-Ann Petrie who was living in Kingskettle at the time, sent me a story from the local Kettle newspaper about the old families of Kettle. One of those families was the Swans.

High Street, Freuchie

In a previous chapter, I talk about my great-grandfather, John Petrie marrying Barbara Swan. Barbara was born in Freuchie, Fife as were her siblings: Robert Swan (1844-) who married Agnes Paterson; William Swan (1844-) who married Isabella Law; Helen Swan (1850-1928) who married James Dowie; David Swan (1852-) who married Margaret Robertson; Alexander Swan (1855-1867); John Swan (1856-);

Walter Swan (1859-); James Swan (1861-1907) who married Elizabeth Anderson; and Janet Swan (1863-).

Barbara's brother James immigrated to Toronto with the Petries in 1904. Four of her nephews also moved to North America in the early 1900s. Robert Swan, son of her brother William moved to Winnipeg in 1902. Her brother Robert's sons: Andrew Swan moved to Toronto in 1907; John Swan immigrated to New York in 1887; and Alexander Swan moved to Toronto in 1910.

Barbara's parents, my 2nd great-grandparents were William Swan (1818-1903) and Janet Ness (1820-1871). They both were born and lived all their lives in Freuchie, Fife. William started his working career as a farm labourer and worked at the same job until he was 30 when he went to work as a handloom operator at the Freuchie linen mill. All of his children followed in his footsteps as linen weavers. The Swan family moved into the house previously rented by the Petrie family on Church Street in Freuchie when the Petries moved to Dundee.

The Farm Freuchie

The newspaper article I mentioned above talked about the Swan family who farmed land known as Riggs Farm just east of Freuchie. The farm was first established in 1664 and was continually owned by Swans until 1866 with the death of Alexander Swan. Known for its prize pigs, this was the farm where my 2nd great-grandfather, William Swan worked. I cannot make a genetic link between my great-grandfather and the pig farmers but it's quite a coincidence. The farm is still an active concern to this day.

Janet Ness's family had lived in Freuchie for at least four generations and were all linen weavers.

William Swan's parents, my 3rd great-grandparents were Robert Swan (1777-1841) and Helen Dawson (1791-1856). They were both born and

Millfield Road, Freuchie

lived all their lives in Freuchie. They had three children and all worked as linen weavers using a handloom in their home.

Helen Dawson's family had also been weavers and originally came from Argyllshire, a county in western Scotland.

Robert Swan's parents were from the town of Dunfermline, Fife and moved around Fife for the first couple of years after their marriage eventually settling in Freuchie about 1775. My

Freuchie Cottages 1850

4th great-grandparents were Robert Swan (1703-) and Margaret Bogie (Boggie) (1705-). Together they had one child, my 3rd great-grandfather. Records show that Robert had four other children by a different wife before marrying Margaret.

Robert's parents, my 5th great-grandparents were David Swan (1670-) and Isobell Mudie (Moodie) (1678-). They were both born and lived all their lives in Dunfermline. They had nine children, all born in Dunfermline.

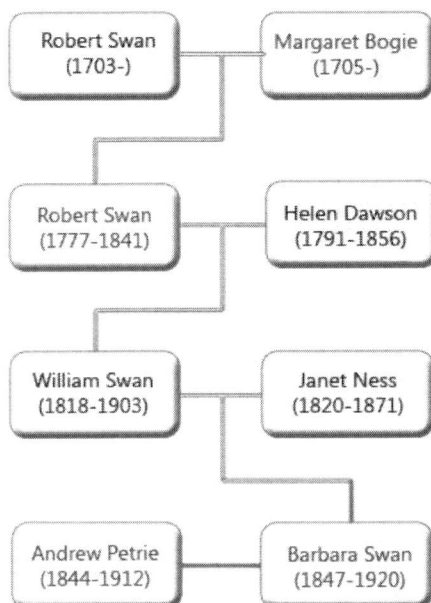

EPISODE 24

THE MUDIE FAMILY

Dunfermline is an ancient town in the southern part of Fife, just 3 miles north of the Firth of Forth and was at one time the royal capital of Scotland. The earliest known settlements in the area date as far back as the Neolithic or Stone Age period, about 12,000 years ago. The area came to prominence during the Bronze age and the first recorded history is from the 11th century when Malcolm III, King of Scots married Saint Margaret from Hungary in the church at Dunfermline. Margaret established a new church under their son King David I. In 1128 it evolved

Dunfermline Palace and Abbey

into an abbey and as part of Dunfermline Palace became the mausoleum of the Scottish Crown. Over the years a total of 18 Scottish royals, including seven kings, were buried here from Queen Margaret in 1093 to Robert Stewart, Duke of

Albany in 1420. King Robert I also known as Robert The Bruce was the last of the seventh Scottish Kings to be buried here in 1329. An interesting bit of Scottish history but also a hint about where the family roots are buried.

Mudie

My 5th great-grandfather, David Swan married Isobell Mudie in 1710. The name Mudie also written as Moodie, Moudie, Mouidie, Muidie and Muday comes from the old English word "modig", which means courageous or brave. There is reason to believe that this is one of the oldest lowland families in Scotland. The family comes from Norwegian descent and first appears in the Orkney Islands. There are 20 recognized branches of the family in Scotland that can prove their relationship to each other along with ties to the royal house of Stewart and King Robert The Bruce.

Our branch of the family is known as the Dunfermline/Masterton branch and goes back eight generations from Isobell Mudie to William Moodie, my 13th great-grandfather who was born in Edinburgh in 1483 and died in Masterton (just outside of Dunfermline) in 1535. The Mudies were landowners and merchants and moved in the higher levels of society at the time. Of course, they did.

Isobell Mudie's parents were Robert Mudie (1652-) and Janet Brown(e) (1659-), my 6th great-grandparents.

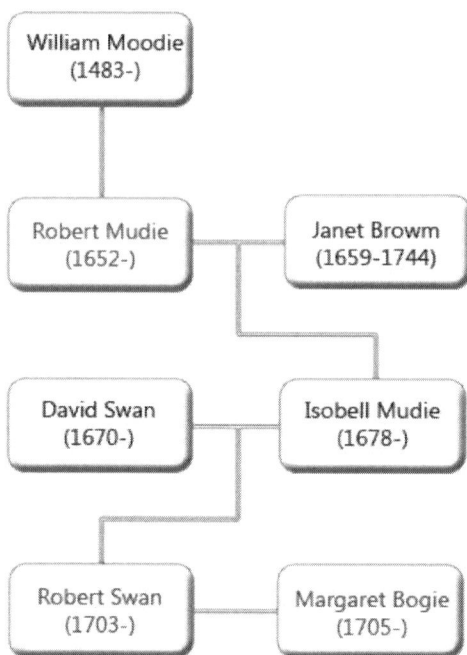

EPISODE 25

CARNEGIE

N o, I'm not claiming Andrew Carnegie as a relative. I looked really hard but could not find even a close link, except one.

Andrew Carnegie (1835-1919) was a Scottish-American industrialist and philanthropist. He was born in Dunfermline, Fife to a poor family in a one-room weaver's cottage on

Carnegie Birthplace, Dunfermline

Moodie Street. In 1836, the family moved to a larger house (four rooms) on Edgar Street.

At the age of 12 in 1848, Carnegie with his parents immigrated to the United States. Carnegie started work as a telegrapher, and by the 1860s had investments in railroads, railroad sleeping cars, bridges and oil derricks. He accumulated further wealth as a bond salesman, raising money for American enterprise in Europe. He built

Pittsburgh's Carnegie Steel Company, which he sold to J.P. Morgan in 1901 for $303,450,000 which would have been around $65 billion today. Surpassing John D. Rockefeller, this made Carnegie the richest man in America for many years.

Carnegie devoted the rest of his life to large scale philanthropy with special emphasis on local libraries, world peace, education, the arts and scientific research. With the fortune he made from business, he built Carnegie Hall in New York and founded the Carnegie Philanthropic

Andrew Carnegie

Corporation of New York, Carnegie Endowment for International Peace, Carnegie Institute for Science, Carnegie Trust for Universities of Scotland, Carnegie Hero Fund, Carnegie Mellon University and the Carnegie Museums of Pittsburgh among others. In fact, by the time he died he had given away almost ninety percent of his fortune.

When David Swan married Isobell Mudie in 1710, Dunfermline had been in decline since 1624 when most of the town was destroyed by fire. However, by the end of the century, the town was showing signs of prosperity with the introduction of the weaving of linen damask. By 1710 Dunfermline had become a centre for the linen trade and the Swan family moved into a newly rebuilt weaver's cottage on Moodie Street. Now could this have been the same cottage that was occupied by the Carnegie family 125 years later? A long shot, but possible.

EPISODE 26

~⋅⟨P⟩⋅~

A MARTYR

Janet Brown, my 6th great-grandmother was born to James Brown (1620-) and Janet Philip (Whiteford) (1628-) of Dunfermline, my 7th great-grandparents. Janet had previously been married to a Mr. Whiteford and James had been married to Elizabeth (Bessie) Beattie. James and Janet had a total of eight children.

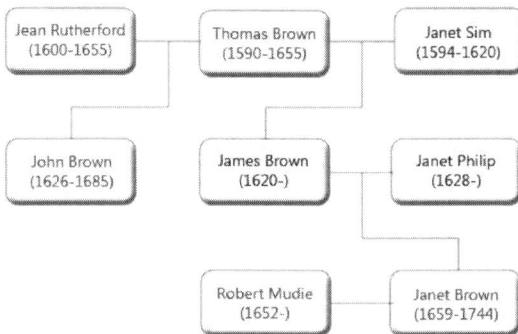

```
Jean Rutherford ─── Thomas Brown ─── Janet Sim
  (1600-1655)        (1590-1655)      (1594-1620)

John Brown          James Brown ─── Janet Philip
  (1626-1685)         (1620-)         (1628-)

Robert Mudie ─── Janet Brown
  (1652-)          (1659-1744)
```

James Brown had a half-brother, John Brown (1626-1685) who became one of the first martyrs for the Presbyterian church. Born and raised at Priesthill farm near Muirkirk in Ayrshire, John was known at the "Christian Carrier" and a Protestant Covenanter.

John Brown

He was educated by Presbyterian ministers who had been deposed by Charles I and had sought refuge among the residents of this rural area where they would travel house to house teaching the gospel. In later years, when the priests had been driven out, John taught a weekly class of religious instruction for the young men of the area. The classes were well attended and John became a spiritual leader to many. He earned his living farming and as a packhorse carrier for local merchants. He was married twice and had one daughter, Janet and two sons, John and James.

At the time, there was an ongoing conflict between the king, Charles II and the Presbyterian church. Those not agreeing with the king were known as Covenanters. John did not participate in any of the uprisings of the Covenanters but felt he had the right to live in peace and practice his religion as he saw fit. The law at the time required everyone to attend the Episcopal curate which was a way of showing support for the king. John refused to attend and his name was added to the list of enemies of the crown. On May 1, 1685, he was arrested at his farm and asked why he would not attend the curate and pray for the king. He replied that "only Christ was the supreme head of the church and the curates were placed there contrary to Christ's law." He then fell to his knees praying loud and fervently and bid farewell to his family. John Graham of Claverhouse, commander of the troops sent to arrest John ordered his men to fire. They refused and, in a

Death of John Brown

rage, Graham drew his own pistol and shot Brown dead. He thus became a Presbyterian martyr in 1685.

James Brown's parents were Thomas Brown (1590-1655) and Janet Sim (1594-1620), my 8th great-grandparents. They both were born and lived in Dunfermline. The Brown family has most often been associated over the years with land ownership and service to the crown. In particular, the Brown family owned vast lands in Fifeshire mainly around Fordell, Finmount and Vicarsgrange.

EPISODE 27

THE BROWN LINE

The Brown Family is an interesting side branch of my family. This is a quick two-hundred-year dash through their history.

You will recall, Thomas Brown, my 8th great-grandfather from the last episode. His parents were John Brown of Priesthill (1575-1631) and Jean Lockheart (1575-1635), my 9th great-grandparents. They farmed at Priesthill in Ayrshire, southwest of Edinburgh.

John Brown's parents were Johnne Brown (1550-1607 and Janet Bell (1553-1618) my 10th great-grandparents. Johnne Brown had a least three other wives with multiple children. He spent most of his life in Dunfermline.

My 11th great-grandfather, Johnne's father was Sir John Brown of Fordell and Finmount (1530-). In 1554, he married Katherine Melville of Raith (1526-1558) in Fifeshire. She held lands in Perthshire and Clackmannanshire as well as in Fife.

John Brown's second wife was Katherine Boswell of Glasmont and Balmuto in Fifeshire. They had a daughter, Katherine who married into the powerful Oliphant family – connecting the Browns to the earldoms of Erroll and Douglas. Unfortunately, the wealth and titles did not fall to my direct descendants.

Balwearie Castle Ruins

Sir John's father was Sir Robert Brown of Fordell (1480-1540) who in 1515 married the daughter of Sir William Scott of Balwearie, Fife, Lady Catherine Scott (1484-1540), my 12th great-grandparents. Robert inherited substantial lands in Fife and Forfarshire from his father and grandfather.

Sir Robert Brown's parents, my 13th great-grandparents were Sir Richard Brown of Fordell and Arngask (1440-1500) and Elizabeth Arnot (1450-1527), daughter of William Arnot of Barberton, a considerable landowner in Fifeshire. Richard Brown's brother, my 14th great-uncle was George Brown (1434-1514), to some an important individual in the history of Scotland. So, let me tell you more.

George Brown was educated at St. Andrews University in Fife and in Paris. He was ordained in 1464 and became Chancellor of Aberdeen and Rector of Tyninghame in East Lothian. In 1483, he was sent to Rome by the Scottish king, James III. During his time in Rome, Brown became "a very close" friend of Rodrigo Borgia, the Spanish Pope, Alexander VI and this led to his appointment as the Bishop of Dunkeld. George transferred the Fordell estate to his brother Richard, attended the Scottish Parliament, and was involved in numerous public works of the time. In 1494, he was the head of the Scottish Commissioners who concluded a peace treaty with the English. He had a large home in Robertson's Close in Edinburgh where he spent most of his time.

Richard Brown's parents, my 14th great-grandparents were Sir George Brown (1410-1450), Treasurer of the Burgh of Dundee and Johanna Balbirny (1420-1440).

Records of the Brown family, also known as Browne or Broun continue back to 1261 with Richard Brown, my 19th great grandfather who was a Magistrate of Elgin in Morayshire during the reign of King Alexander III – a period of frequent Viking attacks on Scotland's coastline including Morayshire.

There are two notable distant Brown cousins. George Brown  (1818-1880) was born in Alloa, Clackmannanshire, just west of Dunfermline, Fife. In 1837, the family immigrated first to New York City and then to Toronto in Upper Canada. George became a newspaper publisher and started The Toronto Globe and Mail. He also was the founder of the Liberal Party of Canada and a Father of Canadian Confederation. His grave in the Toronto Necropolis is a few blocks from where I now live.

James Gordon Brown (1951-) is a British politician who was Prime Minister of the United Kingdom and Leader of the Labour Party from 2007 to 2010. He also served as Chancellor of the Exchequer from 1997 to

Gordon Brown

2007. Brown was a Member of Parliament first for Dunfermline East and later Kirkcaldy and Cowdenbeath, both traditional lands owned by the Brown family centuries before.

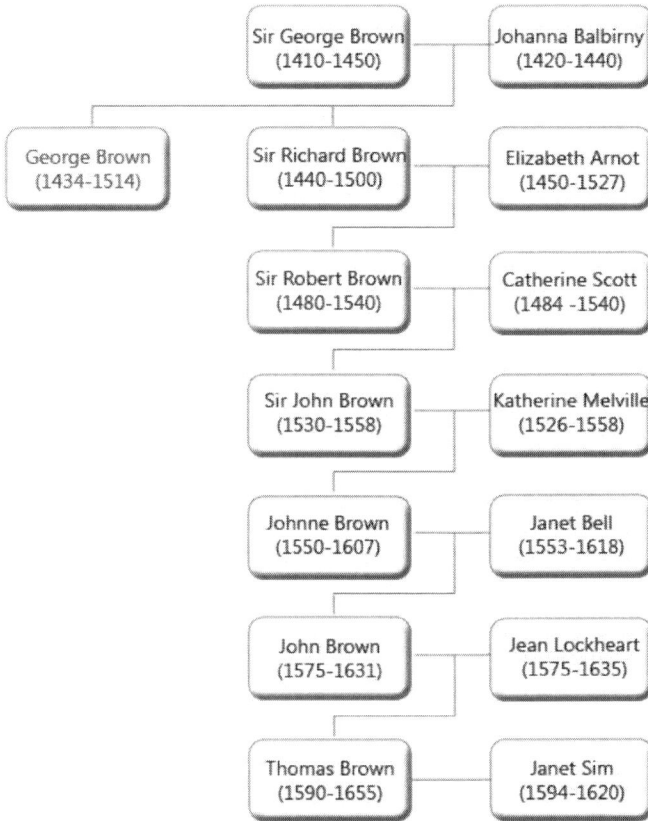

EPISODE 28

✦P✦

THE PHILIP GENERATION

Now we jump back a bit to Janet Philip (Whiteford) and her husband, James Brown who were my 7th great-grandparents. The chart below shows how we got from Barbara Swan to the Philips. Janet Philip's parents, my 8th great-grandparents were William Philipe (1593-1668) and Elspet Lindsay (1601-).

Fingask Castle

William Philipe was the son of Steven Philip(e) (1565-1594), the baillie or magistrate of St. Andrews and his wife Elizabeth Forret of Fingask (1565-). William was Laird of Fingask and Largo as well as a soldier in the English army. He travelled frequently between Scotland and Sweden eventually rising to the rank of Colonel. His wife Elizabeth died sometime around 1631 and William remarried a Swedish woman named Marta Christersdotter Maneskold of Seglinge. They had four sons.

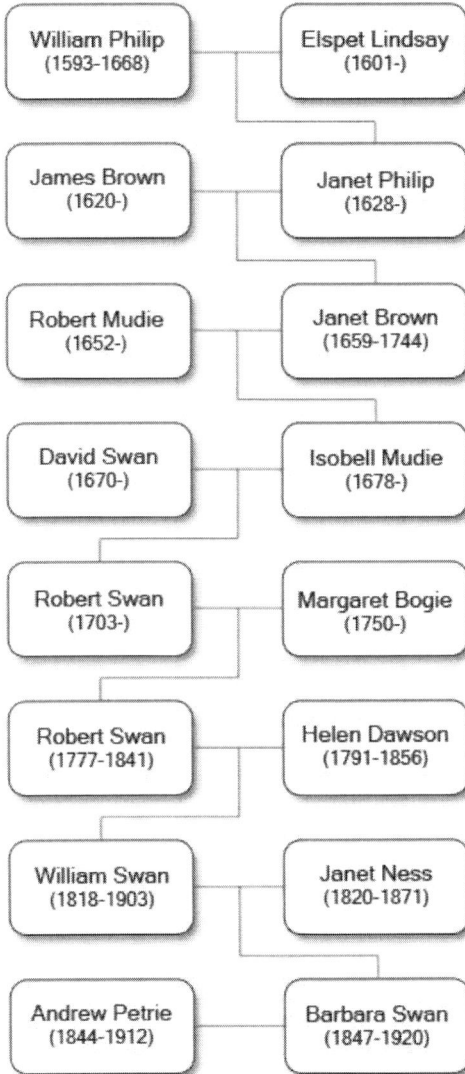

William Philip (1593-1668)	Elspet Lindsay (1601-)
James Brown (1620-)	Janet Philip (1628-)
Robert Mudie (1652-)	Janet Brown (1659-1744)
David Swan (1670-)	Isobell Mudie (1678-)
Robert Swan (1703-)	Margaret Bogie (1750-)
Robert Swan (1777-1841)	Helen Dawson (1791-1856)
William Swan (1818-1903)	Janet Ness (1820-1871)
Andrew Petrie (1844-1912)	Barbara Swan (1847-1920)

EPISODE 29

THE LINDSAY LINK

Elspet Lindsay's parents were Alexander Lindsay, Bishop of Dunkeld (1561-1639) and Barbara Bruce (1565-1628), my 9th great-grandparents. The history of the Lindsay part of the family goes back at least 300 years from this point. I will not talk about every generation, just those of particular interest.

Alexander Lindsay graduated from St. Leonard's College, St. Andrews and in 1591 became Minister of St. Madoes Church in Perthshire. He rose to the rank of Moderator of the Presbytery of Perth and then in 1607 to the position of Bishop of Dunkeld. You may recall that my 14th great-uncle, George Brown had also been Bishop of Dunkeld in the 1400s.

In 1624, Alexander was admitted to the Scottish Privy Council. However, he later became opposed to the introduction of the Book of Common Prayer contrary to royal policy and was demoted back to being the Minister of

St. Madoes Church. Barbara Bruce died in 1626 and Alexander married again to Nicola Dundas.

My 10th great-grandparents were John Lindsay, Laird of Evelick (1537-1599), Alexander's father and Marjory Pitcairn (1540-1605). John was a member of the younger branch of the Lindsay clan, the earls of Crawford. Finally, a part of the family that lived in castles. Sadly, most are now in ruin.

Kirkforthfar Castle Ruins

John Lindsay's parents were David Lindsay (1511-1592) and Helen Crichton (1515-1576), my 11th great-grandparents. They lived at Kirkforthar Castle, just west of Markinch, Fifeshire. Ruins of the house still stand in a farmer's field. Although once surrounded by a moat, no trace now remains.

My 12th great-grandparents were Sir John Lindsay, Master of Lindsay (1482-1525) and Elizabeth Lundie (1490-). John was born in Byres Castle, Haddington, East Lothian but before his death, they moved to Pitcruvie Castle in Fifeshire. Elizabeth Lundie had been married to David Lundie before marrying John in 1521. She was the daughter of Sir Robert Lundie of Balgonie and Jean Lindsay.

John Lindsay's parents, my 13th great-grandparents were Patrick Lindsay, 4th Lord Lindsay of the Byres (1439-1526) and Lady Isabella Pitcairn (1456-1526). Patrick Lindsay was an advisor to James IV of Scotland and counselled the king to fight in the battle of Flodden in 1513 where he fought alongside the king. Unfortunately, the king was killed in the battle. However, in December 1513, Patrick was appointed counsellor to James IV's widow, Queen Margaret Tudor. In 1524, Lord Patrick was appointed High Sheriff of Fife.

Isabella Pitcairn was the daughter of Henry Pitcairn of Pitcairn and Forthar. I cannot find any record of her mother's name.

My 14th great-grandparents were John Lindsay, 1st Lord Lindsay of the Byres (1402-1482) and Agnes Stewart (1410-1477). Lord Lindsay was alive during turbulent times in Scottish history. He was a Privy Counsellor for Scotland and in 1424 was used by his father-in-law, Robert Stewart as a hostage for the ransom of King James I by the English crown. In recognition of his service to the crown, he was created 1st Lord of Lindsay of the Byres in 1444. He later held the offices of Justiciar of Scotland and Lord of Sessions.

Agnes Stewart's parents were Robert Stewart, 1st Lord Lorn and Lady Joan Stewart whose grandfather was King Robert II of Scotland.

The Lindsay family lived at Byres near the medieval market town of Haddington in East Lothian, Scotland. Byres Castle dates back to the 1200s when it and all the lands around were owned

Byres Castle Ruins

by the Dunbar family. In the late 1300s, the land had passed to the Lindsay family for services to the crown. The original castle was rebuilt and expanded several times but was eventually dismantled to build other homes nearby. All that remains today is a two-storey tower house that was within the walls of the original castle.

I will not bore you with all the details of the next several hundred years. However, the Lindsay line goes back to the early 1200s with William de Lindsay, my 20th great grandfather. From 1422 to 1233 the Lindsay's held a variety of positions in service of the Scottish crown including Custodian of Edinburgh Castle, Ambassador to England, Member of the Scottish Parliament, High Chamberland and Regent. For all this service they received land, titles and wealth.

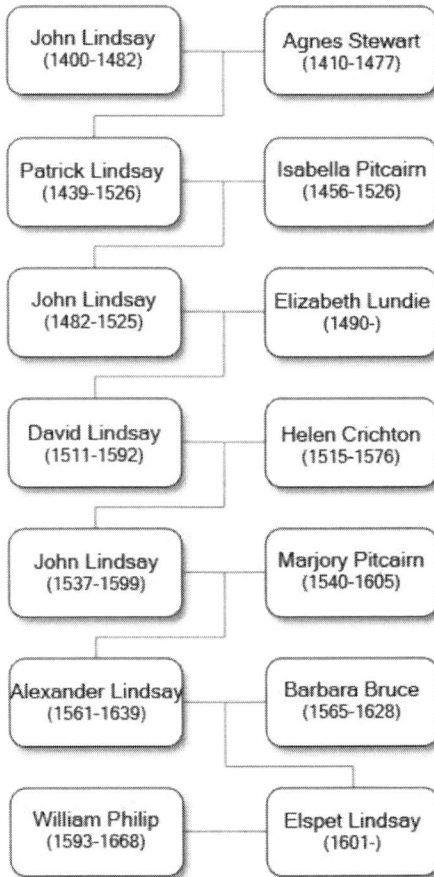

```
John Lindsay          Agnes Stewart
(1400-1482)           (1410-1477)
        |_____|
                |
Patrick Lindsay       Isabella Pitcairn
(1439-1526)           (1456-1526)
        |_____|
                |
John Lindsay          Elizabeth Lundie
(1482-1525)           (1490-)
        |_____|
                |
David Lindsay         Helen Crichton
(1511-1592)           (1515-1576)
        |_____|
                |
John Lindsay          Marjory Pitcairn
(1537-1599)           (1540-1605)
        |_____|
                |
Alexander Lindsay     Barbara Bruce
(1561-1639)           (1565-1628)
        |_____|
                |
William Philip        Elspet Lindsay
(1593-1668)           (1601-)
```

EPISODE 30

❦

BRUCE FAMILY

Now we jump back a few centuries to visit the Bruce branch of the family with the marriage of Bishop Alexander Lindsay (1561-1639) and Barbara Bruce (1565-1628), my 9th great-grandparents.

Barbara Bruce's parents were William Bruce of Fingask and Rait (1535-) and Helen Hay (1555-), my 10th great-grandparents. The Bruce family were descendants of the Bruces of Clackmannan. They lived in Fingask Castle on the lands of Rait which they owned from the 15th century. The castle had been an abbey going back to 1114. The Bruce family lost Fingask in 1671. Laird Laurence Bruce, whose "pecuniary involvements necessitated the sale of the estate for the behoof of his creditors." In other words, he was

Fingask Castle

forced to sell to pay his debts. Fingask Castle is now a popular wedding venue with one of the top-rated gardens in Scotland.

Helen Hay's parents were Peter Hay, 4th of Megginch (1528-1596) and Margaret Ogilvy (1532-1596, my 11th great-grandparents. Peter's father was Sir Peter Hay, 3rd of Megginch (1499-1565) and his mother was Lady Margaret Crichton (1504-), my 12th great-grandparents. More about the Crichtons in a later episode. The Hay family lived in Megginch Castle in Perth and Kinross in central Scotland which was "modernized" by Peter 3rd of Megginch while he was Chamberlain to

Megginch Castle

the monastery at Scone. In 1664, the Hay's sold the castle to the Drummond family who owns it to this day. The castle grounds were used for the filming of the movie Rob Roy.

EPISODE 31

OGILVY FAMILY

Grandma Margaret Ogilvy, my 11th great-grandmother was a descendant of the clan Ogilvy which originated in Angus around 1163. It's an important branch of the family so thought I should spend a few paragraphs talking about their history.

In 1296, my 20th great-grandfather, Sir Patrick de Ogilvy (1280-) swore allegiance to the English king, Edward I in his conquest to take over Scotland. His sons, Sir Patrick Ogilvy (unknown birth and death date), my 19th great grandfather and Sir Robert de Ogilvy (unknown birth and death date) joined forces with Robert the Bruce (also a relative you'll hear about later) to defend Scotland from the English at the Battle of Bannockburn in 1314. As a reward for his faithful service, Patrick received a charter for the lands of Kettins (an area in Perth and Kinross, 11 miles northwest of Dundee). His brother Robert Ogilvy is described as one of the closest friends of Robert the Bruce.

104

In 1365, the Ogilvys became hereditary Sheriffs of Angus and a Sir Patrick Ogilvy commanded the Scottish forces that fought alongside Joan of Arc against the English. For this, he was given the title "Vicomte d'Angus.

Now, we skip a few generations to Sir Walter Ogilvy of Auchterhouse (1360-1392), my 17th great-grandfather who was appointed as High Treasurer of Scotland, a senior post in the Scottish court. He was

Auchterhouse Castle

also Ambassador to England and attended Princess Margaret of Scotland on her marriage to the French Dauphin, heir to the French throne.

Sir Walter Ogilvy's youngest son, Alexander Ogilvy of Auchterhouse (1375-1422), my 16th great-grandfather, unfortunately, did not inherit any of the titles and lands as had his other siblings. He controlled Auchterhouse Castle, just north of Dundee in Angus. He was unmarried but had at least one son, Sir Andrew Ogilvy of Inchmartine (1400-1461), my 15th great-grandfather. He

Inchmartine House Today

acquired Inchmartine House, several miles southwest of Dundee in Perthshire through his marriage to Marjorie Glen (1405-).

Sir Andrew's son was David Ogilvy of Inchmartine (-1506), my 14th great grandfather and his son was James Ogilvy of Balgally and Inchmartine (1460-1513), my 13th great-grandfather. James was killed in the Battle of Flodden Field in 1513. The battle was between England and Scotland and resulted in an English victory. The Scots were led by King

James IV who was also killed in the battle. It is estimated that nearly 10,000 Scots were killed.

James Ogilvy's son was Sir Patrick Ogilvy of Inchmartine (1485-1535), my 12th great-grandfather and his daughter was Grandma Margaret Ogilvy as mentioned above.

David Ogilvy

David Ogilvy, 13th Earl of Airlie (1926-) is the current Chief of Clan Ogilvy and served as Lord Chamberlain to the Queen (Elizabeth II). His brother, Angus Ogilvy married HRH Princess Alexandra of Kent, granddaughter of King George V and Queen Mary.

EPISODE 32

BACK TO THE BORTHWICKS

Now we'll take a step back to the Lindsay clan again and my 11th great-grandparents David Lindsay (1511-1592) and Helen Crichton (1515-1576). Helen's parents were Sir James Crichton of Frendraught (1479-1530) and Catherine Borthwick (1467-1528), my 12th great-grandparents. I want to tell you a little about the Borthwicks.

Catherine's father was Sir William Borthwick, 4th Lord Borthwick (-1542) and Margaret Hay (birth and death date unknown), my 13th great-grandparents. Sir William succeeded his father Sir William Borthwick, 3rd Lord Borthwick who died in 1503. The 4th Lord was named guardian of the infant King James V after his father, James IV was killed during the Scottish defeat at the Battle of Flodden in 1513. The 4th Lord was instrumental in negotiating the peace treaty with England following Flodden. He was appointed Governor of Stirling Castle and immediately had it fortified in anticipation of another conflict with England.

The 3rd Lord Borthwick (1435-1503), my 14th great-grandfather, was Master of the King's Household and a guarantor in several of the treaties with England. The name of his wife is unknown. His parents were Sir William Borthwick, 2nd Lord Borthwick (1420-1483) and Catherine Sinclair (1415-1473), my 15th great-grandparents. The second Lord was an ambassador to England as well as Master of the Household to King James III.

The 1st Lord Borthwick, Sir William of Borthwick (1370-

Borthwick Tomb

1458) was married three times. The names of his first and third wives are unknown but his second wife was Mariota Hoppringle (birth and death date unknown), my 16th great-grandparents. The 1st Lord was a Lord of Parliament which is similar to today's cabinet minister. In 1430 he built Borthwick Castle and the title of Lord Borthwick was granted by King James II around 1437.

The Borthwick family is believed to have come from Hungary in 1057 during the reign of Malcolm III of Scotland. The family seat is Borthwick Castle located 12 miles south-east of Edinburgh in the village of Borthwick. It is one of the largest and best-preserved surviving medieval Scottish fortifications.

The castle was built by the 1st Lord Borthwick and added to by his immediate successors. It provided a refuge for Mary Queen of Scots before being sent to the Tower of London by her sister Queen Elizabeth. The castle is well fortified and only once was captured. In 1650, Oliver Cromwell's

Borthwick Castle

forces took the castle after firing only two cannon shots at the 14-foot-thick walls. During World War II the structure was used as a hiding place to store national treasures. The castle is still the home of the Borthwick clan but is now used as an events venue. Do you think they would welcome long lost relatives for a visit?

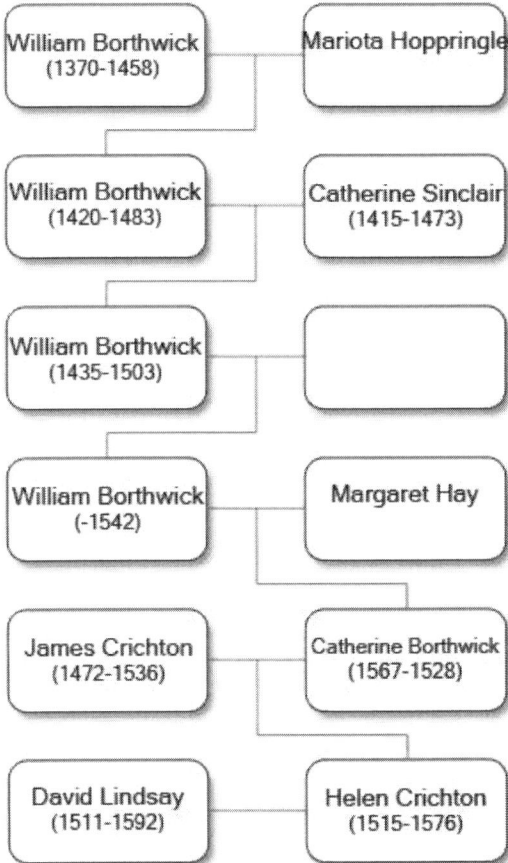

William Borthwick (1370-1458) — Mariota Hoppringle

William Borthwick (1420-1483) — Catherine Sinclair (1415-1473)

William Borthwick (1435-1503)

William Borthwick (-1542) — Margaret Hay

James Crichton (1472-1536) — Catherine Borthwick (1567-1528)

David Lindsay (1511-1592) — Helen Crichton (1515-1576)

EPISODE 33

⊸❦P❧⊷

CRICHTON CONNECTION

You may recall that my 12th great-grandparents were Sir James Crichton and Catherine Borthwick. I've discussed the Borthwick side, now a bit about the Crichtons.

The Crichtons are an ancient Scottish family, but their origins are unknown. They derived their surname from the barony of Crichton, in the county of Edinburgh. A Thurston's de Crichton is one of the witnesses to the charter founding the Abbey of Holyrood in the days of King David I. The family appear to have remained in the rank of minor barons, taking no prominent role in public affairs till near the middle of the 15th century with the birth of my 15th great-grandfather, Sir William Crichton, 1strd Lord Crichton.

The son of John Crichton, William Crichton was one of the first Scottish noblemen given safe passage to England to meet James I of Scotland who had just been released from captivity by the English. William was knighted at the coronation of King James in 1424 and was made Gentleman of the Bedchamber.

In 1426, William was sent to Norway to negotiate a continuation of the peace between Scotland and Norway. Upon his return, he was appointed Governor of Edinburgh Castle, Master of the Royal Household and Sheriff of Edinburgh.

Edinburgh Castle

In 1437, King James I was assassinated and succeeded by his six-year-old son, James II. William Crichton, as Keeper of Edinburgh proclaimed himself Lord Chancellor of Scotland and protector of the young king, in 1439.

Archibald Douglas, 5th Earl of Douglas had been appointed regent until King James II came of age. During this time there was non-stop conflict between William Crichton and Douglas. In 1440, Douglas died and Crichton made his move to ensure the demise of continuing influence by the Douglas clan. He invited the 16-year-old William Douglas, 6th Earl of Douglas (Archibald's son) and his younger brother to dinner in Edinburgh Castle to supposedly negotiate a truce. Instead, he had the boys murdered, despite the pleas of young James II to spare them. This brutal incident became known as the "Black Dinner" and apparently was an inspiration for the "Red Wedding" massacre in the Game of Thrones TV series.

Black Dinner

In 1448, the king had forgiven William for the Douglas murders and sent him to France to ratify the ongoing alliance between Scotland and France. There was no better way to strengthen that alliance than to arrange a marriage for the yet unmarried James II. In 1449, William returned with Mary of Guelders, niece of the Duke of Burgundy as the future Queen of Scotland.

William Crichton's son was Sir James Crichton, 2nd Lord Crichton (1408-1469). He married Lady Janet Dunbar (1416-1506), my 14th great-grandparents. Janet's sister Elizabeth was the wife of Archibald Douglas, as discussed previously. They lived

Crichton Castle

in Crichton Castle which his father had spent great sums on in order to modernize. Not sure what that meant, but it certainly wasn't central heating and indoor plumbing.

They had a son, William Crichton, 3rd Lord Crichton (1455-1493), my 13th great-grandfather. He first married Marion Livingston, daughter of James Livingston, Lord Livingston of Callendar. The wedding was designed to end a long-standing rivalry between the two families. However, their relationship fell apart when Marion had an affair with King James III. Not to be outdone, William had an affair with the King's sister, Princess Margaret Stewart (1450-1512), my 13th great grandmother. There has been much confusion as to whether William and Margaret actually married. During this time William Crichton was also part of a conspiracy to overthrow James III, partly out of revenge for his first wife's unfaithfulness. He was also said to have fortified Crichton Castle against a possible attack by the king. There were at least two, probably a few more children produced from these marriages.

Sir Walter Scott in his writings about the times reports that despite all the palace intrigue and various factions pushing their sides to the history of the day, William and Margaret were in fact married and that James Crichton of Frendraught (1472-1530), my 12th great-grandfather was their son.

The attempt to depose James III was not successful and William Crichton as a result forfeited much of his power and titles.

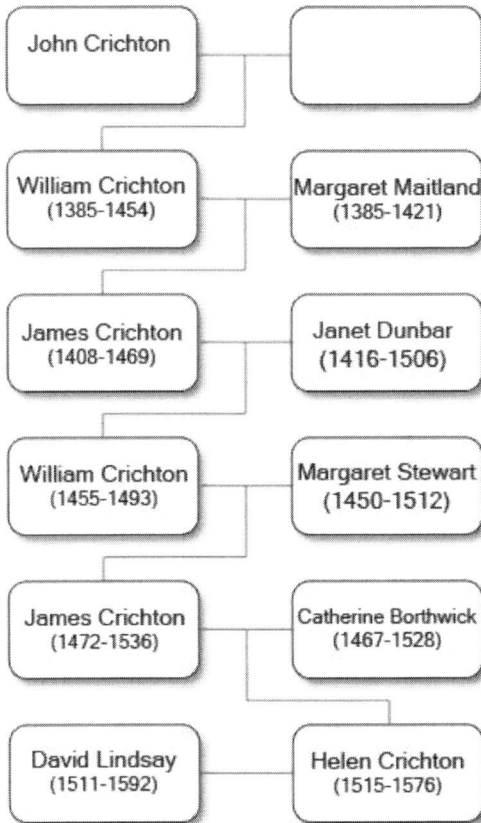

```
┌─────────────────┐         ┌─────────────────┐
│ John Crichton   │         │                 │
│                 │         │                 │
└─────────────────┘         └─────────────────┘

┌─────────────────┐         ┌─────────────────┐
│ William Crichton│         │ Margaret Maitland│
│ (1385-1454)     │         │ (1385-1421)     │
└─────────────────┘         └─────────────────┘

┌─────────────────┐         ┌─────────────────┐
│ James Crichton  │         │ Janet Dunbar    │
│ (1408-1469)     │         │ (1416-1506)     │
└─────────────────┘         └─────────────────┘

┌─────────────────┐         ┌─────────────────┐
│ William Crichton│         │ Margaret Stewart│
│ (1455-1493)     │         │ (1450-1512)     │
└─────────────────┘         └─────────────────┘

┌─────────────────┐         ┌─────────────────┐
│ James Crichton  │         │Catherine Borthwick│
│ (1472-1536)     │         │ (1467-1528)     │
└─────────────────┘         └─────────────────┘

┌─────────────────┐         ┌─────────────────┐
│ David Lindsay   │         │ Helen Crichton  │
│ (1511-1592)     │         │ (1515-1576)     │
└─────────────────┘         └─────────────────┘
```

EPISODE 34

⸮P᷂

THE ROYAL STEWARTS

In the last episode, I mentioned that William Crichton married Princess Margaret Stewart, who was also known as Cecilia, my 13th great-grandparents. Princess Margaret's parents were King James II of Scotland (1430-1460) and Queen Mary of Guelders (1430-1463), my 14th great-grandparents. James was born in Holyrood Abbey along with a twin brother, ten minutes older and therefore heir. However, the brother, Alexander died at the age of one making James the next in line for the Scottish throne. After the assassination of his father, James I, six-year-old James was crowned at Holyrood in 1437.

James II

You may recall from my story about another grandfather, William, 1st Lord Crichton and that the young king was under the control of Crichton and Archibald Douglas, 5th Earl of

Douglas. The two guardians continued to struggle for power through murder and treason until the king reached adulthood in 1449. At that time, he married the niece of the Duke of Burgundy and daughter of the Duke of Gelderland, Mary of Guelders.

By all accounts, James II was popular with his subjects with whom he socialized often. One of his most significant legacies is the founding of the University of Glasgow. His nickname was "Fiery Face" probably due to a large red birthmark on his face which was seen as a sign of a fiery temper, which he had.

James enthusiastically promoted modern artillery for his armies importing cannon from Flanders. During the siege of Roxburgh Castle in 1460, owned by the Douglas clan, a cannon that the king was standing by exploded, killing the monarch.

James I

James I of Scotland (1394-1437), my 15th great-grandfather was King of Scotland from 1406 to 1437. He was born in Dunfermline Abbey, home of the royal household at the time. His older brother and heir to the throne along with a younger brother died under suspicious circumstances. Fears for James, now the heir, and his safety grew and plans were developed to send him to France. On route to France, his ship was attacked by English pirates capturing the prince and delivering him to Henry V of England. Shortly after his abduction, James' father died and the 11-year-old James became the uncrowned King of Scotland. He remained in captivity for another 18 years.

James was well educated in the English court where he was treated as a royal guest rather than a prisoner. He developed a respect for English methods of governance and for King Henry V. James even joined Henry in his military campaign against the French in 1420-21.

In 1416, with the assistance of Henry, James married Joan Beaufort (1407-1445), my 15th great-grandmother, daughter of the English Earl of Somerset. More about Grandma Joan in a later chapter.

Joan Beaufort

Following a series of prisoner swaps and ransoms being paid, James was released in 1424 and returned to Scotland. His re-entry into Scottish affairs was not altogether popular since he had fought alongside Henry V in France sometimes against Scottish forces who were allies with the French. Noble families were required to contribute towards the ransom that was paid to free the king and in some cases, hostages were provided as security until the full ransom was paid. James, who excelled in sporting activities and appreciated literature and music also held a strong desire to impose law and order on his subjects.

To secure his position, James launched a series of attacks on his rivals and critics including those within his own family. Many were executed and others were exiled. He also ignored the plight of the ransom hostages being held in England pending the payment of his ransom monies. James was using the money collected from these families to release their family hostages, for his own grandiose purposes including building a new palace. Opposition grew against James until James was assassinated in 1437 in a failed coup by his uncle, Walter Stewart, Earl of Atholl.

Queen Joan, although wounded in the attack, was able to escape to Edinburgh Castle where her son, now James II was being protected by William Crichton, another 15th great-grandfather as discussed in the last episode.

EPISODE 35

STEWARD TO STEWART

James I's parents were King Robert III of Scotland (1337-1406) and Anabella Drummond (1350-1401), my 16th great-grandparents. Robert was actually born John Stewart and was known for most of his life until he became king at the age of 55 as the Earl of Carrick.

Robert III

John attempted to be helpful to his father in the affairs of the kingdom until his father died in 1390. Now king, but not in good health, his brother, the Duke of Albany was trying to take control. John, now Robert III withdrew to his lands in the west and for a time paid little or no attention to the affairs of state. The only impediment to his brother becoming king was Robert's only surviving son, James. To protect James, he was sent to France at the age of 11 but was captured by the English and held for 18 years, as discussed in a previous episode.

Robert III's parents were King Robert II (1316-1390) and Elizabeth Mure (1320-1355), my 17th great-grandparents. Robert II reigned as King of Scotland from 1371 until he died the first monarch of the House of Stewart. For most of his life, he worked with his uncle, King David II of Scotland but when David died without an heir Robert became king.

Robert II

Not expecting to become king, Robert was having children all over the place, but when it appeared that he might become heir he married Elizabeth Mure and legitimized their four sons and five daughters. A later marriage to Euphemia de Ross in 1355 produced two more sons and two more daughters. Robert died in Dundonald Castle and is buried in Scone Abbey.

Robert II's parents were Walter Stewart, 6th High Steward of Scotland (1296-1327) and Marjory Bruce (1296-1316), my 18th great-grandparents. The title Lord High Steward is that of an officer who controls the domestic affairs of a royal household. Its holders took the surname of Steward and later during the reign of Robert II it became Stewart. An interesting side note, Stewart became known as Stuart in the French court and was often used by monarchs who spent time in France such as James I and VI.

When the 7th High Steward became Robert II, the title was transferred to the eldest male heir of the sovereign. Thus, the Prince of Wales, today is also known as the Prince and Great Steward of Scotland.

Walter Stewart was born at Bathgate Castle in West Lothian, the eldest son of James Stewart, 5th High Steward of Scotland by his third wife, Giles deBurgh, a daughter of an Irish nobleman, Walter deBurgh, 1st Earl of Ulster. Walter fought in the Battle of Bannockburn in 1314 and worked as High Steward in the court of King Robert I of Scotland. He ended up marrying the daughter of the king, Marjory.

Marjory Bruce

Marjorie Bruce was the eldest daughter of Robert the Bruce, King of Scots (1274-1329) and his first wife Isabella of Mar (1277-1296), my 19th great-grandparents.

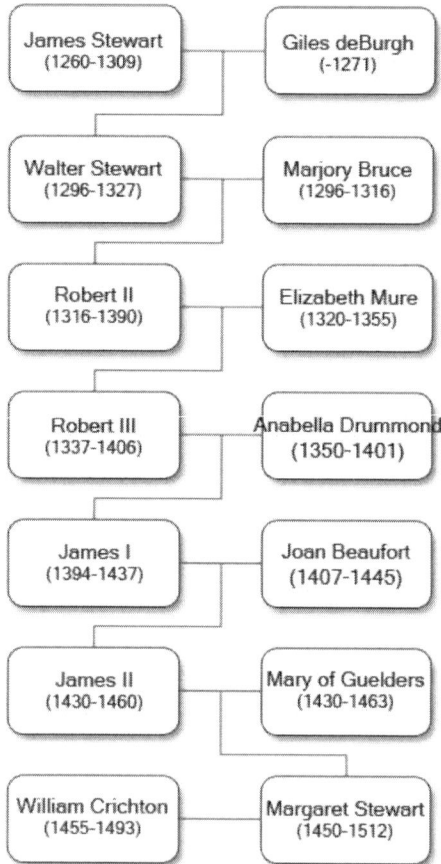

EPISODE 36

ROBERT THE BRUCE

Robert the Bruce (1274-1329) and his first wife Isabella Mar (1277-1296) were my 19th great-grandparents. The story of Robert the Bruce is long and complicated but is the foundation of the modern Scottish royals. So please bear with me as I try to shed a little light on my ancestor's story.

Robert The Bruce

Robert was born into an aristocratic Scottish family. Through his father, he was distantly related to the Scottish royal family. His mother had Gaelic antecedents.

Bruce's grandfather was one of the claimants to the Scottish throne during a succession dispute in 1290. The English king, Edward I, was asked to arbitrate and chose John Balliol to be king. Balliol proved unpopular and in 1296 Bruce joined forces with Edward I to force Balliol to abdicate. Edward then ruled Scotland himself as a province of England.

Bruce then supported an uprising against the English led by

William Wallace

William Wallace. Remember the movie, Braveheart about Wallace. Well, Wallace was defeated and Edward I appointed Bruce a guardian of Scotland along with John Comyn, Balliol's nephew and Bruce's greatest rival. In 1306, Bruce quarrelled with Comyn and stabbed him in a church in Dumfries. He was outlawed by King Edward and excommunicated by the pope. Bruce now proclaimed his right to the throne and on March 27, 1306, was crowned king at Scone. A year later Bruce was deposed by Edward's army and forced to flee. His wife and daughters were imprisoned and three of his brothers executed. Robert spent his time in exile in Northern Ireland.

Returning to Scotland, Robert waged a highly successful guerrilla war against the English. At the Battle of Bannockburn in June 1314, he defeated a much larger English army under Edward II, confirming the re-establishment of an independent Scottish monarchy. Two years later, his brother Edward Bruce was inaugurated as high king of Ireland but was killed in battle in 1318. Even after Bannockburn,

Battle of Bannockburn

Edward II refused to give up his claim to the overlordship of Scotland. In 1320, the Scottish nobility en masse sent a letter to Pope John XXII declaring that Robert Bruce was their rightful monarch. This was known as the "Declaration of Arbroath" and it asserted the antiquity of the Scottish people and their monarchy.

Four years later, Robert received papal recognition as king of an independent Scotland. An old alliance between Scotland and France was renewed, by which Scots were required to make war on England should hostilities break out between England and France. In 1327, the English deposed Edward II in favour of his son and peace was made with Scotland. This included a total reversal of all English claims to superiority over Scotland.

Robert died on June 7, 1329, and was buried at Dunfermline Abbey. He requested that his heart be taken to the Holy Land, but it only made it as far as Spain. It was eventually returned and buried in Melrose Abbey.

I could trace the family back several hundred years further but the records become less reliable and there is only so much history my dear readers can take.

And there we have it from Andrew Petrie to Robert the Bruce. Things my granny never told me.

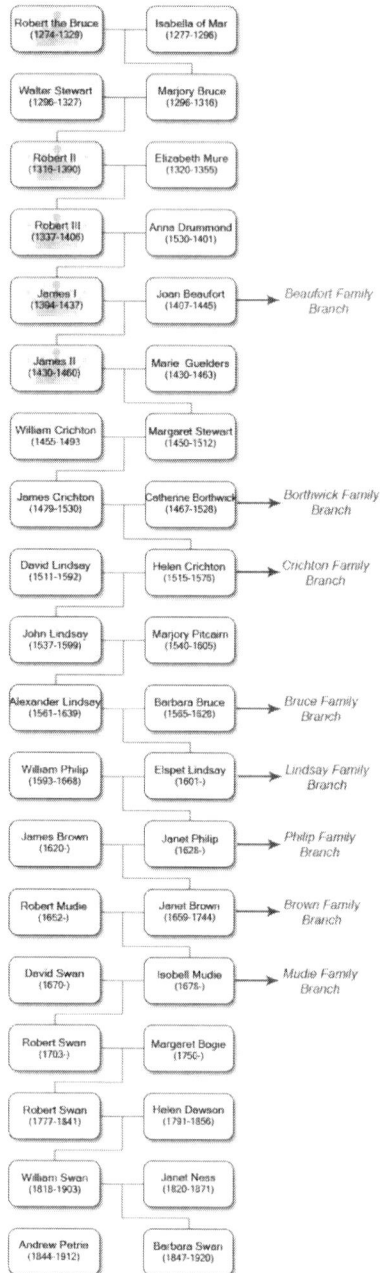

Robert the Bruce (1274-1329)	Isabella of Mar (1277-1296)	
Walter Stewart (1296-1327)	Marjory Bruce (1296-1316)	
Robert II (1316-1390)	Elizabeth Mure (1320-1355)	
Robert III (1337-1406)	Anna Drummond (1530-1401)	
James I (1394-1437)	Joan Beaufort (1407-1445)	Beaufort Family Branch
James II (1430-1460)	Marie Guelders (1430-1463)	
William Crichton (1455-1493)	Margaret Stewart (1450-1512)	
James Crichton (1479-1530)	Catherine Borthwick (1467-1528)	Borthwick Family Branch
David Lindsay (1511-1592)	Helen Crichton (1515-1575)	Crichton Family Branch
John Lindsay (1537-1599)	Marjory Pitcairn (1540-1605)	
Alexander Lindsay (1561-1639)	Barbara Bruce (1565-1628)	Bruce Family Branch
William Philip (1593-1668)	Elspet Lindsay (1601-)	Lindsay Family Branch
James Brown (1620-)	Janet Philip (1628-)	Philip Family Branch
Robert Mudie (1652-)	Janet Brown (1659-1744)	Brown Family Branch
David Swan (1670-)	Isobell Mudie (1675-)	Mudie Family Branch
Robert Swan (1703-)	Margaret Bogie (1750-)	
Robert Swan (1777-1841)	Helen Dawson (1791-1856)	
William Swan (1818-1903)	Janet Ness (1820-1871)	
Andrew Petrie (1844-1912)	Barbara Swan (1847-1920)	

CHAPTER FOUR

THE ENGLISH CONNECTION

EPISODE 37

JOAN BEAUFORT

J ust when you thought we were done, another chapter. This time I want to tell you all about the English Connection to the Petries. I know, you thought we were Scottish through and through. In an attempt to rule over the Scots, the English for years fought in a back and forth struggle for supremacy in the British Isles. At several points, it was thought that love was better than war and English royalty married into Scottish royalty. This is the story of one such encounter.

Let me take you back to my 15th great grandmother, Joan Beaufort. Joan was the daughter of John Beaufort, 1st Earl of Somerset and Margaret de Holland. More about them in the next episode. Joan's claim to fame is that she was married to King James I of Scotland, my 15th great grandfather and mother to King James II of Scotland.

Joan Beaufort

James I

You may recall that King Robert III of Scotland, James I's father, had attempted to send his younger son James Stewart to France to guard him against the machinations of his uncle, Robert, Duke of Albany, but the twelve-year-old James was captured by the English en route to France. When King Robert died soon after, in 1406, James succeeded to the Scottish throne as James I. While the young king grew up in English captivity, his ambitious and self-serving uncle was appointed Regent and Governor of Scotland. His uncle apparently enjoyed this new role and made little effort to negotiate the release of young James. During this time, our family intersected with the Crichton family, notably Sir William Crichton which I've discussed in a previous episode.

Young James received education and travelled with the English court, where he learned about government and administration. These skills he later put to use when he returned to his native Scotland.

Joan met James I during his English captivity around 1420. James fell in love with Joan and wrote her a series of love letters that today apparently still inspire young lovers. While a union between Joan and James was based on love, the English court saw it as a political alliance between the English and Scottish people. It was hoped this would align Scotland with England rather than Scotland's traditional ally, France. They were married in London in 1424. The wedding was widely celebrated by the English court especially with festivities at Winchester Palace hosted by Joan's uncle, the powerful Cardinal Henry Beaufort.

Just before the marriage, James had negotiated his release for a substantial ransom, the Scots had to pay for the return of their King. The couple made their way back to Scotland immediately after the wedding. Joan was crowned Queen of Scotland at Scone Abbey on May 21, 1424. Together they had eight children including James II and Margaret of Scotland, future spouse of Louis XI of France.

Joan was treated as a near equal to her husband and endeavoured to have him demonstrate a reign of mercy and kindness. However, James did manage to get rid of most of his enemies from the Albany Stewarts and the Douglas clan. In 1437, James was assassinated during a coup led by Sir Robert Graham of Perth. Joan was also wounded in a frantic attempt to protect her husband. Joan escaped and was forced to give up any control of the government but remained in charge of her young son, the new king, James II.

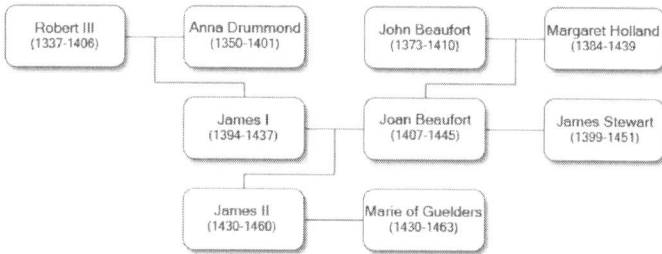

Near the end of 1439, Joan married again. This time to James Stewart, the Black Knight of Lorn and son of the Scottish ambassador to England. The power struggle for control over the country continued with Joan, her new husband James and young King James II being held captive in Stirling Castle. It was there that Joan died in 1445 and her son, James went on to rule Scotland in his own right.

EPISODE 38

THE HOLLANDS

My 16th great grandfather is John Beaufort, the eldest son of John of Gaunt Plantagenet and his mistress Katherine Swynford. Beaufort's surname (properly de Beaufort) reflects his birthplace at his father's castle of Beaufort in the Champagne region of France. He served King Richard II and also his own half-brother, Henry IV. This is starting to sound like a Shakespeare play. John was born in 1373 and was raised to be a warrior and a champion jouster. In 1397, he was created an earl becoming the 1st Earl of Somerset, Marquis of Dorset and Lord High Admiral of England.

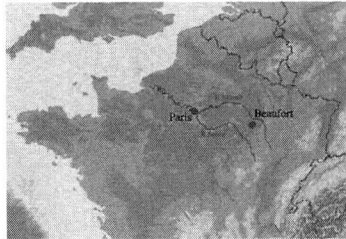

John married Lady Margaret Holland, my 16th great grandmother. Margaret was the daughter of Thomas Holland, 2nd Earl of Kent and Alice FitzAlan. John and Margaret had six children including Joan Beaufort as previously discussed in another episode.

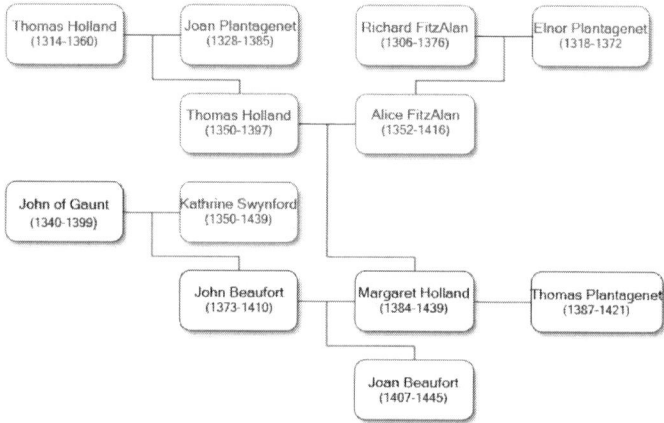

Margaret was invested in the Order of the Garter in 1399. In 1410, Beaufort died and a year later she married Beaufort's nephew, Thomas of Lancaster, Duke of Clarence, the son of King Henry IV. They had no children. Margaret died in 1439 and is buried along with her two husbands in a carved alabaster tomb in Canterbury Cathedral that shows her lying between the two of them.

Margaret Holland and Husbands

Thomas Holland, my 17th great grandfather was born in Upholland, Lancashire in 1350. He was the eldest surviving son of Thomas Holland, 1st Earl of Kent and Joan Plantagenet who was known as "The Fair Maid of Kent". In 1360 upon the death of his father, Thomas became Baron Holland.

On April 10, 1364, Thomas married Lady Alice FitzAlan, daughter of Richard FitzAlan, 10th Earl of Arundel and his wife, Eleanor Plantagenet of Lancaster. They had four sons

Richard FitzAlan

and six daughters. All of the sons died without legitimate heirs, whereupon the daughters and their children became co-heiresses to the House of Holland.

Thomas was appointed captain of the English forces in Aquitaine in 1366 and for ten years fought various battles with the French. He was made a Knight of the Garter in 1375. He died in 1397 at Arundel Castle.

Arundel Castle

EPISODE 39

PINUP GRANNY

The life of my 18th great-grandmother, Joan Plantagenet or Joan of Kent was marked by frequent, sudden change and was full of adventure. If she lived today, she would be known as the pinup granny. She was born in 1328, the third child and second daughter of Edmund of Woodstock, Earl of Kent and Margaret Wake of Liddell. She was of royal blood, as her father was the sixth son of King Edward I of England. However, when Joan was just two her father was beheaded for treason. Once her cousin, Edward III took control of the kingdom, Joan was made welcome into his court where she was raised. By her early teens, Joan had become a strikingly attractive woman and began to be known as "the fair maid of Kent". One chronicler of the time referred to Joan as "the most beautiful woman in the whole world and the most amourous." Apparently, she fell in and

Joan of Kent

132

out of love many times and welcomed the attentions of the many young knights at Edward's court. Her portrait adorned many a knight's lodgings.

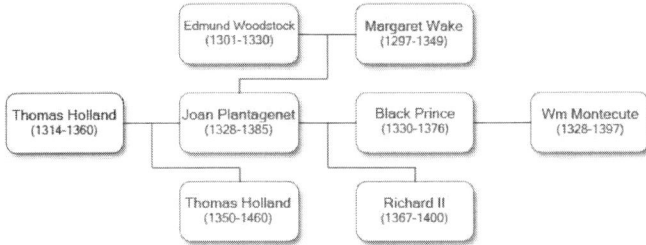

When she was 15 or 16, she was the subject of a dispute between two prospective husbands, William de Montacute, Earl of Salisbury and Sir Thomas Holland. Holland seems to have won out. However, shortly after they were married, Holland was called away to war in France and Salisbury forced Joan into a contract for marriage. Once Holland returned, he appealed to the Pope to have Joan restored to him, he won the case and Joan returned as his wife in 1349.

In 1352, Joan inherited the title of Countess of Kent, following the deaths of her older siblings, becoming a very wealthy woman as a result. In 1360, Holland died leaving Joan with five young children. However, only a few months later she was engaged to the King's eldest son, Edward, Prince of Wales also known as the Black Prince. Evidently, Edward had been in love with Joan since they were children. The marriage was delayed while a Papal dispensation was obtained because the two were related and the King was godfather to Joan's sons. The couple went on to have two sons, one of whom eventually became King Richard II of England. When Edward died, Joan played a pivotal role in guiding her son, Richard and remained active in English politics until she died in 1385.

EPISODE 40

─◦§P§◦─

EDMUND OF WOODSTOCK

My 19th great-grandfather was Edmund of Woodstock, Earl of Kent.

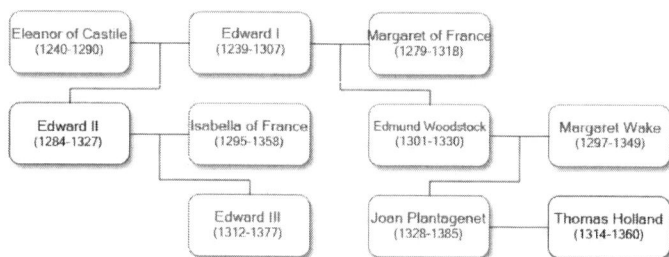

King Edward I of England had a great many children by his first wife, Eleanor of Castile, but only one son survived into adulthood – the future Edward II. After Eleanor died, the King married Margaret of France, with whom he had two children. Thomas and when the King was 62, Edmund. Edmund was born at Woodstock in Oxfordshire in 1301 and was therefore referred to as Edmund of Woodstock. Son of the English king, he was also, through his mother, grandson of King Phillip III of France.

Edward II

Edward I had intended to make substantial grants of land to young Edmund, but when the King died in 1307, Edmund's half-brother, now King Edward II failed to follow through on his father's wishes. Instead, the new king gave the land and titles to his male lover, Piers Gaveston. Although he did grant Edmund the lesser title of Earl of Kent. Edmund nevertheless, remained loyal to his half-brother and played an important part in his administration, acting as a diplomat and military commander. He even helped suppress several rebellions against the king. Discontent with Edward continued to grow especially as he lavished rewards and titles on his new boyfriends. At some point, Edmund had enough and joined a rebellion that

Edward II and Piers Gaveston

successfully ousted the king and replaced him with a young Edward III. Edmund soon fell out of favour with the new court and was caught planning a new rebellion. He was beheaded without a trial by the court. When Edward III came of age and assumed personal control of the government, he annulled the charges against his uncle and returned his lands and titles to his children. Unfortunately, there was nothing that could be done about reattaching his head.

EPISODE 41

EDWARD I

Edward I Plantagenet, King of England was my 20th great-grandfather. He was born in 1239, the son of Henry III and Eleanor of Provence. At the age of 15, he married the 9-year-old Spanish Princess, Eleanor of Castile. Edward's early adulthood took place against a backdrop of civil strife between his father and rebel barons.

Edward I

Edward was 6'2", considered very tall for the time which earned him the nickname "Longshanks". He was temperamental, and along with his height, made him an intimidating man, instilling fear in his contemporaries.

In 1270, Prince Edward left England to join the Eighth Crusade. His father died while he was away and Edward returned to London in 1274 for his coronation. The first part of his reign was dominated by his campaigns in Wales. He invaded Wales in 1277, defeated the Welsh leader, Llywelyn ap Gruffyd and built a ring of castles to enforce his authority over the Welsh people. Wales was brought into the English legal and administrative framework and in 1301 Edward's eldest son was proclaimed Prince of Wales – a tradition that continues to this day.

At home, Edward was responsible for a variety of legal and administrative reforms, asserting the rights of the Crown, promoting the uniform application of justice and codifying the legal system of common law. His military campaigns necessitated increases in taxation which in turn required more regular meetings of parliament – by the end of Edward's reign, these had become an established part of political life. The desire for financial gain by the crown contributed to Edward's expulsion of Jews from England in 1290. All of their assets including debts owed to them became the property of the king. This edict lasted for almost 350 years.

In 1292, Edward was asked to arbitrate in a succession dispute in neighbouring Scotland and Edward nominated John Balliol as Scottish king. Balliol swore allegiance to Edward, but Edward's ongoing demands pushed the Scots into an alliance with France. Edward was not amused and invaded Scotland. Opposition to the English gathered around William Wallace, but he was captured and executed in 1305. In 1306, the Scottish nobleman, Robert the Bruce rebelled. You may recall in a previous chapter that Bruce was also my 19th great-grandfather. However, Edward I and Bruce never faced each other in battle. Edward died on his way to Scotland in 1307. Robert the Bruce went on to defeat the English forces at the Battle of Bannockburn confirming an independent Scottish monarchy. Edward is buried in Westminster Abbey.

EPISODE 42

～❦P❦～

HENRY III

My 21st great-grandfather was also King of England, Henry III. Henry was born on October 1, 1207, the son of King John and Isabella of Angouleme. He assumed the throne when he was only nine years old and was helped in his reign by several regents, one of whom, was William Marshall a 70-year-old knight who had loyally served the Plantagenet family for decades. When Henry was crowned the country was in the midst of a rebellion known as the "First Barons War". After several battles, Henry promised the barons that he would abide by the provisions of Magna Carta also known as the Great Charter of 1225.

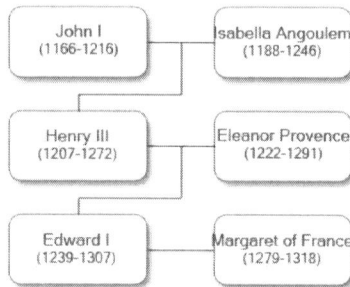

```
┌──────────────────┐        ┌──────────────────┐
│ John I           │        │ Isabella Angoulem│
│ (1166-1216)      │────────│ (1188-1246)      │
└──────────────────┘        └──────────────────┘
          │
┌──────────────────┐        ┌──────────────────┐
│ Henry III        │        │ Eleanor Provence │
│ (1207-1272)      │────────│ (1222-1291)      │
└──────────────────┘        └──────────────────┘
          │
┌──────────────────┐        ┌──────────────────┐
│ Edward I         │        │ Margaret of France│
│ (1239-1307)      │────────│ (1279-1318)      │
└──────────────────┘        └──────────────────┘
```

Henry III

His reign was marred with further rebellions by the barons and failed attempts to regain French territories lost by his father. Henry travelled less than previous monarchs, investing heavily in a handful of his favourite palaces and castles. He married Eleanor of Provence, with whom he had five children. Henry was known for his Christian piety, holding lavish religious ceremonies and giving generously to charities. However, he also extracted huge sums of money from the Jews in England, ultimately crippling their ability to do business. His actions hardened public opinion against Jews resulting in the issuance of the Statute of Jewry which segregated the Jewish community. This anti-Jewish attitude would continue into the reign of his son Edward I.

Despite his many shortcomings, Henry ruled for 56 years, a record not surpassed until the reign of George III in 1816. He put his seal to Magna Carta willingly in 1225, which was unchanged since his father, King John first agreed to it in 1217. By the end of his reign, it was enshrined as the bedrock of English values. He established Britain's first parliament. He rebuilt Westminster Abbey into the form we know it today. He started the pageantry we now associate with current royal events. He encouraged his queen to play an active role in state affairs and was known as a faithful husband and adoring father.

Henry's willingness to make peace and pursue international diplomacy was beneficial for education, art and trade. Under his rule, construction and craftmanship flourished, Oxford and Cambridge Universities grew to maturity and "the wine coming in and wool going out" made England among the richest countries in Europe.

Henry believed it was his duty as a ruler to make sure his subjects were fed. He personally provided food for hundreds daily and thousands on special occasions. When famine hit in the 1250s, the starvation of his people could only mean there was something wrong with his rule and he had to fix it through a series of reforms. Admitting mistakes and forgiving transgressions became hallmarks of his reign.

Henry III Tomb, Westminster Abbey

Henry III died in 1272 and is buried in Westminster Abbey. After his death, attempts were made to have him made a saint, but he was never canonized.

EPISODE 43

KING JOHN

When I discovered that my ancestors inspired the tales of Robin Hood, I imagined men running around Sherwood Forrest in tights robbing from the rich, etc. Well, not quite. The evil King John of Robin Hood fame was my 22nd great-grandfather. John ruled England from 1199 to 1216. John was given the nickname "Lackland" by the royal court because unlike his older siblings he was not granted any lands or title by his father. The son of Henry II of England and Eleanor of Aquitaine, John succeeded his older brother Richard I, also known as Richard the Lionheart. In 1200, John married Isabella of Angouleme and they had five children including his heir, Henry III. If you recall the Robin Hood saga, John was always scheming, assisted by the Sheriff of Nottingham, to take over the crown from his brother Richard while he was

John I

away fighting a crusade. While partially true, John has gone down in history as one of the worst kings ever to sit on the English throne, both for his character and his failures. He lost the Angevin-Plantagenet lands in France and so crippled England financially that the barons rebelled and forced him to sign the Magna Carta in 1215.

John's Seal on Magna Carta

This charter, Magna Carta, limited royal power and emphasized the primacy of the law overall, including the monarchy. However, the king and the barons mostly ignored the terms of Magna Carta for the remainder of his reign. It wasn't until his son Henry III reaffirmed the edict in 1225 that it came into force.

John continued to battle the barons who invited Prince Louis, son of the future Louis VIII of France to be their king. A civil war broke out, often called the First Barons' War which would not end until the reign of Henry III. During the fighting, John caught a fever and died on October 18, 1216. He was just 48. The dead and unlamented king was buried in Worcester Cathedral, as requested in his will.

EPISODE 44

HENRY II

Henry II of England ruled from 1154 to 1189 and was my 23rd great-grandfather. He came to the throne of England by negotiations with his predecessor, King Stephen of England following a civil war that had raged between Stephen and Henry's mother Empress Matilda. Henry was born as Henry of Anjou in 1133, the son of Geoffrey, Count of Anjou and Matilda, the daughter of Henry I of England. Matilda gained her title of Empress from a previous marriage to the Holy Roman Emperor, Henry V. She married Geoffrey in 1128 who became known by his nickname, "Plantagenet" because his family coat of arms featured the broom plant.

Henry II

Henry II was known for his good looks, intelligence, and ability to speak several languages. Credited with boundless

energy and drive, the king was of stocky build, piercing grey
eyes, red hair and a ferocious temper. In later life, he
apparently developed a significant paunch. Sounds like a lot
of my other relatives.

Henry inherited his father's lands in Normandy, Anjou,
Touraine and Maine, but was ambitious for much more.

Eleanor of Aquitaine

Following military victories in
Brittany and his marriage to
Eleanor of Aquitaine in 1152, the
former wife of Louis VII of
France, Henry came to control
most of France. Henry wanted
more, to control England,
weakened by years of civil war. He
and Eleanor would have eight
children including the future King Richard I and King John,
the Robin Hood kings.

Henry began a new ruling dynasty, the Angevins-
Plantagenets, formed the largest empire in western Europe
and established himself as one of England's greatest kings.
His reign however is marred by two events: the rebellion by
his sons against him and the murder of Thomas Becket.

The 1160s for Henry were dominated by Henry's relationship
with Thomas Becket. Henry wanted to exert his control over
the church and in 1161 appointed Thomas Becket, who was
at the time his chancellor, to the position of Archbishop of
Canterbury. In Henry's eyes, he thought this would place him
in charge of the English church and he would be able to
retain power over Becket. However, the Archbishop seemed
to change in his role and became a defender of the church
and its traditions. He consistently opposed and quarrelled
with Henry not allowing him to dictate to the church. By
1170 their relationship had deteriorated even further and
while at court, the king is supposed to have said, "someone

rid me of this turbulent priest."
These words were taken to
heart by a group of four
knights who proceeded to
murder Becket in front of the
high altar at Canterbury
Cathedral. This event caused

Murder of Becket

shockwaves throughout Christian Europe and has tended to
overshadow the great things Henry managed to achieve.

Even though his last few years as king were tormented by
disputes with his sons over how the empire would be divided
between them, Henry's legacy remains proud. His empire-
building laid the foundation for England and later, Britain's
ability to become a global power. His administrative changes
remain embodied in church and state to this day.

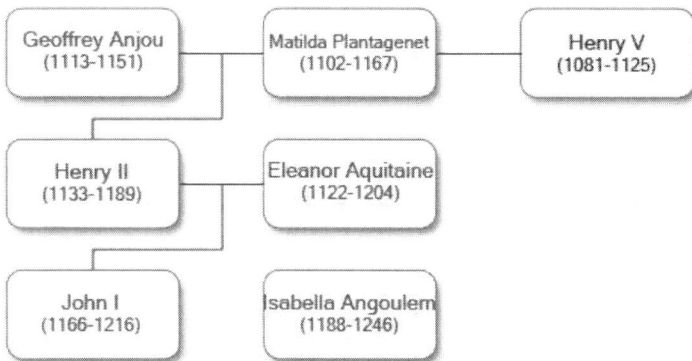

EPISODE 45

MAUDE

My 24th great-grandmother was Empress Matilda. She lived from 1102 to 1167 and was known by her supporters as Empress Maude. Despite being a claimant to the English throne and years of plotting, intrigue and fighting, it never happened.

Empress Matilda

Matilda's father, Henry I of England fathered a record number of illegitimate children, at least 23, but no one knows for sure. He did, however, have two legitimate offspring, Matilda born in 1102 and William Aelin in 1103. Naturally, the male would become the heir. Catastrophe hit in 1120 when William was drowned crossing the English Channel. Aside from a personal tragedy, Henry now had a political crisis on his hands. He remarried in an attempt to have another male heir but there were no legitimate children born. This left Matilda as the only heir to his throne. Fearful of the reaction of a misogynistic nobility

Henry had to do something to bolster support for Matilda. So, he married her off to Henry V, the Holy Roman Emperor and forced the nobles to swear loyalty to the Empress.

In 1125, Henry V died and three years later the now 26-year-old Matilda was forced by her father to marry again. Her new husband was Geoffrey, son of the Count of Anjou, who was just 15 and merely a count's son, something Matilda resented as beneath her imperial status. Matilda remained unpopular in the Anglo-Norman courts and when her father, Henry died in 1135 she faced open

Henry V

opposition from the barons. The throne instead was given to Matilda's cousin, Stephen of Blois, who enjoyed the backing of the English church.

Stephen de Blois

Not satisfied to remain the runner-up and exiled to France, in 1139 Matilda crossed to England to challenge Stephen by force. For two years, the two sides fought numerous battles with Stephen being captured by Matilda's forces in 1141. Matilda rushed to London in an attempt to have herself crowned but was met with angry opposition from the mob. The church declared that Matilda could never be formally declared Queen of England but rather was given the title, "Lady of the English". Stephen was later exchanged for her half-brother, Robert and resumed his role as king. The war between the two sides degenerated into a stalemate, with Matilda controlling much of the south-west of England, and Stephen the south-east and midlands. The rest of the country fell into the hands of the local barons.

147

In 1148, Matilda gave up and turned over the battle to her eldest son, Henry who continued the fight until 1154 when Stephen recognized Henry as next in line to the throne. Henry was eventually crowned as Henry II, forming the Angevin Empire.

Matilda retired to Normandy and spent the rest of her life providing advice to her son and working with the church where she founded the Cistercian monasteries.

EPISODE 46

HENRY I

Another Grandpa as king. My 25th great-grandfather was Henry I of England. He lived between 1068 and 1135 and ruled from 1100 until 1135. Henry was the fourth son born to William the Conqueror and Queen Matilda of Flanders. He was the only son born in England.

Robert Curthose

Henry was raised for a life in the church and was educated in Latin and the liberal arts. Upon his father's death in 1087, Henry's two older surviving brothers were each left with half of their father's kingdom. Robert Curthose became Duke of Normandy and William Rufus King of England. But poor Henry, still a minor, was left with no inheritance. When he grew older, he tried to buy land from his brothers and struggled to build himself a power base in the Cotentin peninsula in western Normandy. He eventually allied himself with his brother William against their brother

Robert. In 1100, while hunting with Henry, William was killed, shot with an arrow. Some say it may not have been an accident. At the same time, brother Robert was away fighting on a Crusade. Henry wasted no time in rushing to London to seize the throne for himself.

William Rufus

A year later, Robert has returned from the crusades, invaded England in an attempt to capture the crown from Henry but was forced by the barons to retreat to Normandy wherein 1106 he was defeated by Henry's forces and held prisoner by his brother for the rest of his life.

Henry I

As king, Henry made many social reforms. He issued the Charter of Liberties which is considered to be a predecessor of the Magna Carta. He restored many of the popular laws of Edward the Confessor. His reign marked a significant advance from personal monarch towards a more bureaucratic state. The role of exchequer was developed to deal with royal revenues and royal justices began to tour the counties to reinforce local administration and collect taxes, often quite aggressively.

Henry was married twice. Matilda of Scotland was his first wife and Adeliza of Louvain his second. He is rumoured to have had at least 23 illegitimate children and only two by Matilda. After his death, the crown passed to his nephew Stephen and then his grandson, Henry II.

EPISODE 47

⚜️P⚜️

WILLIAM WON

Now we come to the end of my story. Well actually, it's the beginning point for most school children to learn about modern British history. Although the history of Britain goes back over many thousands of years, William the Conqueror, my 26th great-grandfather is where the story of Britain begins for many.

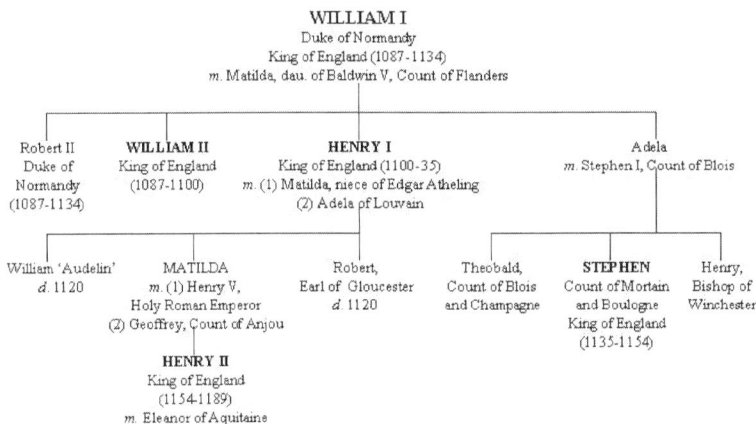

WILLIAM I
Duke of Normandy
King of England (1087-1134)
m. Matilda, dau. of Baldwin V, Count of Flanders

Robert II	**WILLIAM II**	**HENRY I**	Adela
Duke of Normandy (1087-1134)	King of England (1087-1100)	King of England (1100-35) m. (1) Matilda, niece of Edgar Atheling (2) Adela of Louvain	m. Stephen I, Count of Blois

| William 'Audelin' d. 1120 | MATILDA m. (1) Henry V, Holy Roman Emperor (2) Geoffrey, Count of Anjou | Robert, Earl of Gloucester d. 1120 | Theobald, Count of Blois and Champagne | **STEPHEN** Count of Mortain and Boulogne King of England (1135-1154) | Henry, Bishop of Winchester |

HENRY II
King of England
(1154-1189)
m. Eleanor of Aquitaine

William was born in 1028, the illegitimate son of Robert I,

Robert, Duke of Normandy

Duke of Normandy and a woman called Herleva, the daughter of a local tanner and undertaker. William and other Normans descended from Scandinavian invaders who pillaged northern France in the late ninth century. William's father died while on a crusade to Jerusalem in 1035. Eight-year-old William became the new Duke of Normandy. Violence and corruption plagued his early reign, as the feudal barons fought to control his fragile dukedom. However, with the help of King Henry I of France who knighted William in 1042, William survived and finally gained control of his duchy.

In 1051, William married Matilda of Flanders, a granddaughter of France's King Robert II. She rejected him when they first met, perhaps because of his illegitimacy and her involvement with another

William and Matilda

man at the time. According to legend, the snubbed William tackled Matilda in the street, pulling her by her hair to a nearby haystack and having his way with her. It must have worked because she agreed to marry him and bore him ten children before her death in 1083.

In the meantime, the childless king of England, Edward the Confessor, whose mother was a sister of William's grandfather promised William succession to the English throne. However, when Edward died in 1066, his brother-in-law Harold Godwin, claimed the throne of England for himself. William, angered by the betrayal, decided to invade England and claim his throne.

William assembled a massive invasion force but was delayed from sailing for weeks by bad weather. Meanwhile, the Norwegian army invaded England in the north. Harold quickly moved his forces north to defend England from Norway. After defeating the Norwegians, Harold quickly marched his troops back south in anticipation of the Norman invasion. Unfortunately, they were not given time to rest and on October 14, the English and Norman armies met at the now-famous Battle of Hastings. King Harold was killed by an arrow through the eye and then was hacked to pieces. At the end of the battle, no leadership remained for the English forces leaving the way clear for William to march on to London where he was crowned King of England on Christmas Day 1066.

Battle of Hastings

There were several revolts in the next five years, which William used as an excuse to confiscate English land and declare it as his personal property. He then distributed the land to his Norman followers, who imposed their unique feudal system. Eventually, Normans replaced the entire Anglo-Saxon aristocracy. William, however, retained most of England's institutions and was intensely interested in learning as much as he could about his new property and people. This resulted in the compilation of the first-ever census known as the Domesday Book.

William the Conqueror

William's opponents had freely called him William the Bastard which they reluctantly had to change to William the Conqueror after the Battle of Hastings. William was also illiterate and spoke only French which he imposed on the new English court. French was then used as the official court language for centuries completely transforming the English language, infusing it with many words we use today. William was apparently also touchy about his appearance and weight. He was described in his early years as "strapping and healthy" but ballooned into just fat in his later life. The king of France likened him to a pregnant woman about to give birth. The corpulent conqueror became so upset with his size that he devised his own fad diet, consuming only wine and spirits for a certain period. It didn't work, but he had fun.

William died in 1087 while on a campaign in northern France. He is buried in the town of Caen, France. Every English monarch who followed William, including Elizabeth II, is considered a descendant of William the Conqueror. Some even say that at least 25 percent of the English population is distantly related to him. Well, now you know that so are the Petries albeit through a more direct line. Again, more things my granny never told me about.

EPILOGUE

I suppose I've always had a thing for the royal family. It's a combination of awe, envy, respect, tradition and history. It's almost as if they are a natural part of my life. My maternal grandparents had a framed picture of King

George VI and
Queen Elizabeth

George VI and Queen Elizabeth, which had been cut out of a commemorative issue of the Toronto Telegram, hanging in their den. As a frequent visitor to their house, we lived just across the street, I used to wonder if my grandparents knew the king and queen, Surely, they must. Why else would they decorate their favourite room in the house with those pictures? My grandfather was a prominent Orangeman and member of the Peel County Conservative Party. I was sure he must know the royals personally.

In grade two, our teacher, Mrs. Cunningham announced one day that the school had arranged a very special treat for all the students at Westacres Public School. The next day we were

going to watch the
coronation of Queen
Elizabeth II. The
following morning all
of the students
assembled in the
auditorium to watch a
National Film Board film of the coronation which had taken
place several years before. It was part of a five-year NFB plan
to show the historic event to every school child in Canada. I
sat beside the projector which Mr. French, the school janitor
was operating. The film was on three giant reels and clicked
away for over an hour. I was mesmerized by the colour,
costumes, marching bands, soldiers and the thousands of
people cheering. This coronation must be a very important
thing in our lives. Why else would the school make sure we
saw it take place. It was then that I started to notice that
pictures of the Queen were everywhere, in every classroom,
at the post office, in the Applewood Acres plaza Dominion
Store and on all of our money. The Royal Family was part of
my life.

In grade eight, I was to make my one and only foray as an
actor. I was cast to play the prince in Mark Twain's, The
Prince and the Pauper. It was a royal role
and I had been picked to play it. As the
curtain closed, I was sitting on the throne
of England wearing my blue velvet
doublet, which our next-door neighbour
Mrs. Aiken made for me along with her
daughter's leotards to the strains of
Mussorgsky's Great Gate of Kyiv. I knew
at that point that I must have royal blood.

In my teen years, one of my many fantasies was that I was an
illegitimate child of the Duke of Edinburgh. Somehow,
Prince Phillip and my mother got together during one of his

many trips to Canada. It was just going to be a matter of time before all was revealed and I was whisked off to London to assume my role as a royal prince. I'm ashamed now that I even thought my mother was capable of such a deed.

I am a year younger than Prince Charles, Prince of Wales and as such felt we were part of the same "modern generation". Perhaps one day we would meet and he would seek my counsel on Canadian affairs. In 1963, the 14-year-old prince, while attending Gordonstoun School in Scotland was spotted by the press sneaking a glass of cherry brandy at a local pub. The story became world news and I was on the verge of writing my kindred spirit with advice on how to avoid the media. I am sure he would have appreciated the input from one of his loyal subjects and friend. Just another royal fantasy.

As I grew up my fascination with the royals continued. I became involved in politics through and following university and gained insight into the importance of the monarch to the Canadian form of government. In April 1982, my political involvement saw me selected as one of a group of young Canadians to be invited to take part in the ceremonies marking the patriation of the Canadian Constitution from Great Britain. Our group comprised of one young person from each of the 282 federal constituencies were the focus of a state dinner for the Queen as part of the constitution celebrations. We were flown to Ottawa from around the country, put up in the brand-new Ottawa Holiday Inn and schooled in royal protocol. On the night before the official signing ceremony on Parliament Hill, we were lined up at the entrance to the hotel banquet hall prepared to be introduced to the Queen. She was accompanied by Prime Minister, Pierre Trudeau and slowly made her way down the line. And then it was my turn. Deep down I hoped she would recognize my true devotion and have a conversation with me. All I got was, "And where are you from?" "Mississauga Mame" and with that, her eyes were already on Steve Podborski, the next person in line. Nevertheless, I was impressed and maybe a little embarrassed by the fact that during my few seconds with the Queen I could not take my eyes off the incredible diamond and emerald necklace she wore. Those stones had to be the size of chicken eggs. How on earth could she keep her head up?

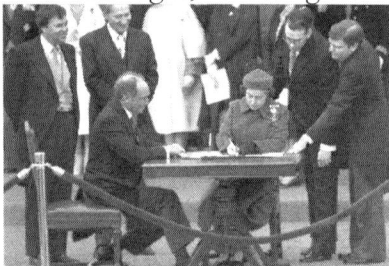

Later that night, following the dinner and departure of the Queen and Prime Minister we continued on dancing and socializing till early next morning. I even had a dance with one of the Queen's Ladies-in-Waiting who had been asked to stand in as the Prime Minister's date for the evening. Apparently, he had been dating the actress, Margo Kidder at the time but she stood him up for the dinner not wanting the publicity that would ensue from dating a married man in such a public way.

Over the years I have maintained my affinity to the royal family. While not going as far as to join the Monarchist League of Canada I do pay attention to royal news and watch all of the big royal events on television. I am drawn to others who have connections with regal folks. In the 1980s I met John Peter Hayden III from New York whose grandmother, he claimed, was a German Duchess, related to Kaiser Wilhelm. Several years later I met a retired American diplomat, Arthur Collingsworth Jr. who told me of his relationship to the Romanov family. He was a godson of Tihon Kulikonsky, son of Grand Duchess Olga Alexandrovna and nephew of Czar Nicholas II of Russia. I was a bit doubtful but when he showed me his collection of hundreds of original watercolour paintings by the Grand Duchess, I was impressed for I too had met her when I was six years old.

The exiled Grand Duchess moved from Denmark to Canada with her family in 1948 to avoid threats to her life from the Soviet Union. She eventually settled on Camilla Drive in Cooksville, Ontario, now part of Mississauga. By this point, she had lost all of her wealth and survived by growing nursery stock behind her modest red brick house. My grandfather, who lived a few blocks away in Cooksville, also grew and sold nursery stock. One day, I accompanied my grandparents on a visit to Olga's to buy some shrubs. While the adults carried on business out back, I stayed inside playing with Lenny, Olga's grandson. I don't remember much about the house or Lenny except the two large, dark portraits of bearded men that hung on either side of the fireplace. I later learned that these were portraits of

Grand Duchess Olga
In Cooksville Home

Olga's father Czar Alexander III and her brother, Czar Nicholas II. I had come close to the remnants of one of Europe's wealthiest royal families and didn't even know it.

Now you will understand why I've taken the time to write my interpretations of the history of the Petrie family. Just to prove that I just might have a wee bit of royal blood in my veins. If only my granny had told me.

PHOTO AND ILLUSTRATIONS CREDITS

I would like to thank and recognize the following sources I used in this book for phots, illustrations and content.

A History of Scotland
Albert Franck
Ancestry.com
BBC.co.uk
Borthwickcastle.com
Brisbanehistory.com
Britannica.com
Britainirelandcastles.com
British Library
Canadian Pacific Archives
Castlesofscotland.co.uk
City of Toronto Archives
Coventer.org.uk
Douglashistory.co.uk
Dundee Heritage Trust
Francisfrith.com
G.M. Gardner
Metropolitan Museum of Art
Monikie.org
National Gallery of Scotland

National Library of Scotland
National Museum of Scotland
National Portrait Gallery
Oldfreuchie.com
Petrie family photos
Punch
Scotland's History
Scotland Info Guides
Scotsman.com
Scottishchurches.org.uk
Stewartsociety.org
The Sons of Scotland
Telegraph.co.uk
Toronto Globe and Mail
Toronto Real Estate Board
Tour Scotland
University of Glasgow
Westminsterabbey.co.uk
Wikimedia & Wikipedia

Printed in Poland
by Amazon Fulfillment
Poland Sp. z o.o., Wrocław